W9-AAF-718

Berklee Practice Method

KEYBOARD

Get Your Band Together

RUSSELL HOFFMANN
PAUL SCHMELING
and the
Berklee Faculty

Berklee Press

Director: Dave Kusek
Managing Editor: Debbie Cavalier
Marketing Manager: Ola Frank
Sr. Writer/Editor: Jonathan Feist
Writer/Editor: Susan Gedutis
Product Manager: Ilene Altman

ISBN 0-634-00651-7

1140 Boylston Street
Boston, MA 02215-3693 USA
(617) 747-2146

Visit Berklee Press Online at
www.berkleepress.com

DISTRIBUTED BY

HAL•LEONARD®
CORPORATION
7777 W. BLUEMOUND RD. P.O. BOX 13819
MILWAUKEE, WISCONSIN 53213

Visit Hal Leonard Online at
www.halleonard.com

DESIGN TEAM

Matt Marvuglio	Curriculum Editor
	Dean of the Professional Performance Division
Jonathan Feist	Series Editor
	Senior Writer/Editor, Berklee Press
Rich Appleman	Chair of the Bass Department
Larry Baione	Chair of the Guitar Department
Jeff Galindo	Assistant Professor of Brass
Matt Glaser	Chair of the String Department
Russell Hoffmann	Assistant Professor of Piano
Charles Lewis	Associate Professor of Brass
Jim Odgren	Academic Advising Coordinator
Tiger Okoshi	Associate Professor of Brass
Bill Pierce	Chair of the Woodwind Department
Tom Plsek	Chair of the Brass Department
Mimi Rabson	Assistant Professor of Strings
John Repucci	Assistant Chair of the Bass Department
Ed Saindon	Assistant Professor of Percussion
Ron Savage	Chair of the Ensemble Department
Casey Scheuerell	Associate Professor of Percussion
Paul Schmeling	Chair of the Piano Department
Jan Shapiro	Chair of the Voice Department

The Band

Rich Appleman, Bass
Larry Baione, Guitar
Russell Hoffmann, Keyboard
Jim Odgren, Alto Sax
Casey Scheuerell, Drums
Paul Schmeling, Keyboard

Music composed by Matt Marvuglio.
Recording produced and engineered by Rob Jaczko,
    Chair of the Music Production and Engineering Department.

Contents

CD Tracks

Foreword

Berklee College of Music has been training musicians for over fifty years. Our graduates go onto successful careers in the music business, and many have found their way to the very top of the industry, producing hit records, receiving the highest awards, and sharing their music with millions of people.

An important reason why Berklee is so successful is that our curriculum stresses the practical application of musical principles. Our students spend a lot of time playing together in bands. When you play with other musicians, you learn things that are impossible to learn in any other way. Teachers are invaluable, practicing by yourself is critical, but performing in a band is the most valuable experience of all. That's what is so special about this series: it gives you the theory you need, but also prepares you to play in a band.

The goal of the *Berklee Practice Method* is to present some of Berklee's teaching strategies in book and audio form. The chairs of each of our instrumental departments—guitar, bass, keyboard, percussion, woodwind, brass, string, and voice—have gotten together and discussed the best ways to teach you how to play in a band. They teamed with some of our best faculty and produced a set of books with play-along audio tracks that uniquely prepares its readers to play with other musicians.

Students who want to study at Berklee come from a variety of backgrounds. Some have great technique, but have never improvised. Some have incredible ears, but need more work on their reading skills. Some have a very creative, intuitive sense of music, but their technical skills aren't strong enough, yet, to articulate their ideas.

The *Berklee Practice Method* teaches many of these different aspects of musicianship. It is the material that our faculty wishes all Berklee freshmen could master before arriving on our doorstep.

When you work through this book, don't just read it. You've got to play through every example, along with the recording. Better yet, play them with your own band.

Playing music with other people is how you will learn the most. This series will help you master the skills you need to become a creative, expressive, and supportive musician that anyone would want to have in their band.

Gary Burton
Executive Vice President,
Berklee College of Music

Preface

Thank you for choosing the *Berklee Practice Method* for keyboard. This book/CD package, developed by the faculty of Berklee College of Music, is part of the *Berklee Practice Method* series—the instrumental method that teaches how to play in a band.

The recording included with this method provides an instant band you can play along with, featuring great players from Berklee's performance faculty. Each tune has exercises and practice tracks that will help prepare you to play it. Rock, blues, and funk are just some of the styles you will perform.

The lessons in this book will guide you through technique that is specific to playing a keyboard instrument in a contemporary ensemble. When you play in a band, your primary concern is with chords—how to read and play them, how to progress from one to the next, and how they interact with other instruments, melodically and rhythmically. This is very different than traditional classical playing, and it will be a major part of this method. This book is intended for keyboard players who know how to read notes and basic rhythms, and play all major scales and some arpeggios. Ideally, this method should be learned under the guidance of a private teacher, but keyboard players learning on their own will also find it invaluable.

Most important, you will learn the skills you need to play keyboard in a band. Play along with the recording, and play with your friends. This series coordinates methods for many different instruments, and all are based on the same tunes, in the same keys. If you know a drummer, guitarist, horn player, etc., have them pick up the *Berklee Practice Method* for their own instruments, and then you can jam together.

Work hard, make music, have fun!

Paul Schmeling
Chair of the Piano Department
Berklee College of Music

Russell Hoffmann
Assistant Professor of Piano
Berklee College of Music

Basics

Before you start chapter 1, you should understand the following topics.

PARTS OF A KEYBOARD

Output Jack
(to amp)

Volume Control

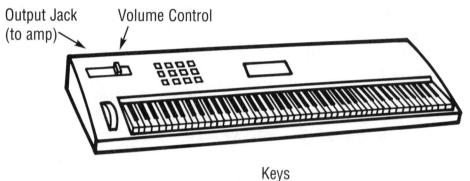

Keys

PLUGGING IN

To protect your equipment and your ear drums, follow these steps when you plug into an amp.
1. Turn off the amp, and set the volume on the amp and the keyboard all the way down.
2. Plug your 1/4" cable into your keyboard and then into the amp.
3. Turn on the amp.
4. Turn up the keyboard volume eighty percent of the way.
5. Slowly, turn up the amp volume until it is loud enough.

Amp

1/4" cable

Output Jack

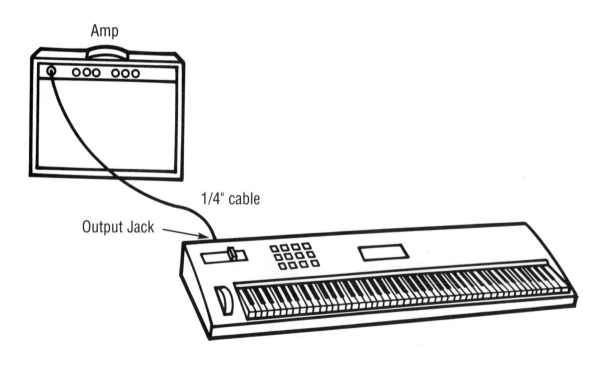

PLAYING POSITION

When you play keyboards, sit up straight, centered at the keyboard. Bend your elbows at right angles, so that your forearms are parallel to the ground and the keys.

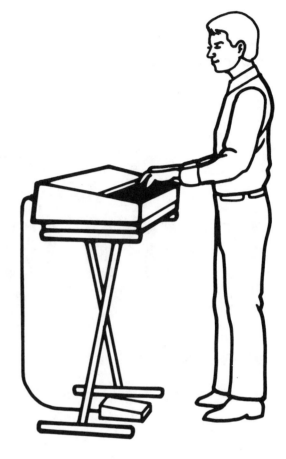

HAND POSITION

Your hands should be relaxed, with your fingers slightly curved.

FINGERINGS

In keyboard work, fingers are numbered like this.

NOTATION

Notes are written on a staff.

Keyboards read from two staffs: treble clef and bass clef. When the staffs are bracketed together, they are called the *grand staff*. Here are the notes for the lines and spaces of the grand staff.

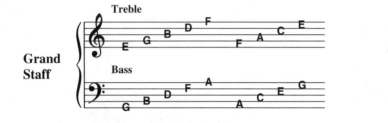

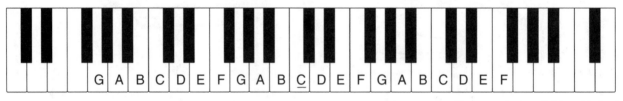

Middle C

LEDGER LINES

The staff can be extended with ledger lines.

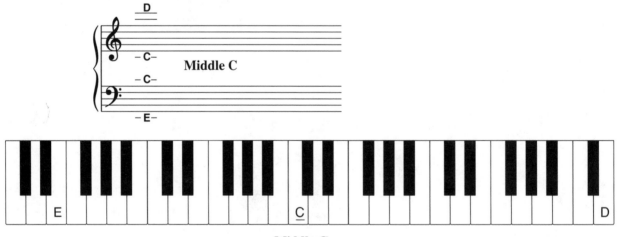

Middle C

ACCIDENTALS

Accidentals are symbols appearing before notes, showing that a pitch is raised or lowered for the duration of the measure, unless otherwise indicated.

♭   Flat   Next note down (half step)

♯   Sharp   Next note up (half step)

♮   Natural   Cancels a flat or sharp

SCALES: MAJOR AND MINOR

Scales are patterns of notes, presented sequentially in a single octave. Two common types of scales are the major and minor scales.

KEY SIGNATURES

Key signatures indicate a tune's key and show which notes always get sharps or flats. Accidentals on the lines and spaces in the key signature affect those notes unless there is a natural sign. Here are some key signatures used in this book.

RHYTHMS

Here are some basic rhythms. When there are no actual pitches, as in a clapping exercise, rhythms may be shown on the *percussion clef*. (The beats are numbered below the staff).

Connect notes using a tie. The first note is held for a total of six beats.

Extend a note's rhythmic value by using a dot. A dot increases the value by one half.

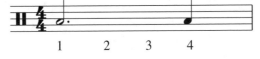

Triplets squeeze three even attacks into the space of two. In this example, the quarter-note beat is divided first into two eighth notes, and then into three eighth-note triplets.

RHYTHMIC NOTATION

Music that just shows rhythms may be written in rhythmic notation. This is common for rhythm exercises when you clap or tap your foot, without sounding any specific pitches.

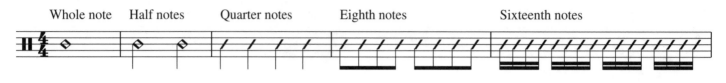

MEASURES

Groups of beats are divided into measures. Measure lengths are shown with *time signatures*.
This measure is in $\frac{4}{4}$ time—there are four quarter notes in the measure.

In $\frac{12}{8}$ time, there are twelve eighth notes per measure.

ARTICULATIONS

Articulations give more information about how to play a note. Here are four common ones used in this book:

>	Accent	Loud
.	Staccato	Short
^	Short Accent	Short and loud
–	Long Accent	Hold for full value

Now, let's play!

"Sweet" is a *rock* tune. Rock started in the 1960s and has roots in blues, swing, r&b, and rock 'n' roll. There are many different styles of rock. To hear more rock, listen to artists such as Rage Against the Machine, Melissa Etheridge, Korn, Paula Cole, Bjork, Tori Amos, Primus, Jimi Hendrix, and Led Zeppelin.

LESSON 1
TECHNIQUE/THEORY

LISTEN **1** PLAY

Listen to "Sweet" on the recording. This tune has two main parts. The keyboard parts are shown below with notes only, no rhythms.

In the first part, the keyboard plays this: In the second part, the keyboard plays this:

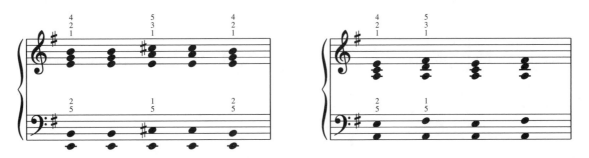

Practice each hand separately before playing both together. Then play along with the recording and try to match the keyboard on the recording. Notice that there is a short introduction before the first part begins.

CHORDS

The keyboard part you just played was made up of *chords* (three or more notes played at the same time). "Sweet" has two kinds of chords: *major* and *minor*. These chords are built using notes of the major or minor scale. In this tune, the chords are *triads* (chords with three notes, besides any octave doublings).

In the first part, the first chord you played was an E minor triad. It is built using the first, third, and fifth notes of the E minor scale.

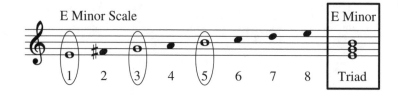

The second chord you played was an A major triad. It is built using the first, third, and fifth notes of the A major scale.

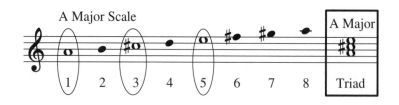

Play the chords along with the first part to "Sweet." Listen to the different qualities of the two chords.

CHORD SYMBOLS

Chords are often represented by *chord symbols*. *Major chords* use just the chord's letter (**A**). *Minor chords* add a long dash (**E–**) to the letter (or sometimes, a lowercase "m" or "min" instead of the dash).

The second part to "Sweet" uses two different chords: A minor and D major.

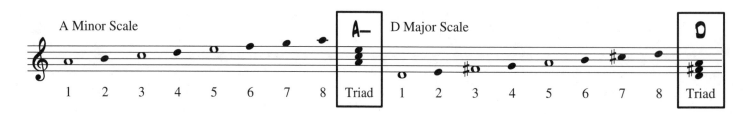

Play along with the second part of "Sweet." Here are the notes and chord symbols.

LEAD SHEETS

When you play in a band, your sheet music might show just chord symbols and melody. This is called a *lead sheet*. Lead sheets tell which chords to play along with the melody. The whole band may read the same lead sheet. Each player will use it differently to create a part for their instrument. As a keyboard player, you will use the lead sheet to learn which chords to play.

This is what the first part of "Sweet" looks like on a lead sheet:

This is what the lead sheet looks like for the second part:

You will see the full lead sheet to "Sweet" in lesson 4.

PERFORMANCE TIP

You may notice that the chord notes next to the scales are stacked in a different order than the chords in the notated parts. Lead-sheet notation lets you decide how to arrange the chord notes. It also lets you choose your own rhythms to play these chords. When you read off a lead sheet, you can play the chords however you want, as long as your part fits in, or *hooks up*, with what the rest of the band is playing.

Different keyboard players will create different parts to the same tune. This is one of the coolest things about lead-sheet notation: it leaves room for individual interpretation.

LESSON 2
LEARNING THE GROOVE

WHAT IS A GROOVE?

A *groove* is a combination of musical patterns in which everyone in the band feels and plays to a common pulse. This creates a sense of unity and momentum. The *rhythm section* (usually drums, bass, guitar, and keyboard) lays down the groove's dynamic and rhythmic feel. A singer or soloist also contributes to the groove and performs the melody based on this feel.

Listen to "Sweet." As is common in hard rock, the groove to "Sweet" has a strong, clear pulse, and a loud, forceful sound. The drums play a heavy, repetitive beat. The bass outlines the harmonic structure. The guitar and keyboards play chords. Everyone uses the same rhythms, though often at different times. This makes the whole band sound like one unit, or *hooked up* with the groove.

In lesson 1, when you played along with the recording and matched the keyboard part, you hooked into a groove and became part of the rhythm section. As you heard in this recording, the keyboard's job in a groove is usually to play chords. This is called *comping*. The part you have been playing to "Sweet" is a comping part.

Listen to the first keyboard comping part played by itself. It is simpler than you might expect. This comping part was created to be played with the other rhythm section parts, which also sound simple, individually. When all the rhythm-section instruments play together, the groove they create sounds interesting. If all individual parts were too complex, the groove would sound muddy.

 **LISTEN 5 PLAY**

Listen to just the bass and keyboard playing the groove. Are they playing the same rhythms or different rhythms?

HOOKING UP TO ROCK

The way to hook up to a groove is by learning its pulse and rhythmic feel. Then, you will be able to play a comping part that hooks up rhythmically with the rest of the band.

LISTEN 2 PLAY

Listen to the first part of "Sweet," and focus on the bass and keyboard. Notice how the keyboard comping part on the recording uses the same rhythm as the bass. The bass line is very prominent in this tune, as it often is in rock. That is one of the reasons that the keyboard is so hooked into the groove—it plays the same rhythms as that driving bass.

LISTEN 2 PLAY

Count along with the beat, repeating "1, 2, 3, 4" through every measure. While you count, tap your right hand along with the snare drum on beats 2 and 4. This is called the *backbeat*. A strong backbeat is one of the characteristics of rock.

Tap				
(Backbeat)		>		>
Count	1	2	3	4
(Pulse)				

 **LISTEN 2 PLAY**

While you tap and count, tap your left hand on the quarter-note pulse, along with your counting.

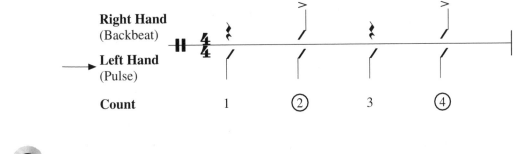

LISTEN 2 PLAY

This tune has a sixteenth-note feel, so change your counting to sixteenth notes, matching the cymbals. On each beat, count evenly, "1 e + a, 2 e + a, 3 e + a, 4 e + a" ("ee and uh"). Try this first at a slower tempo, without the recording, until you get the hang of it. When you are ready, hook up with the recording.

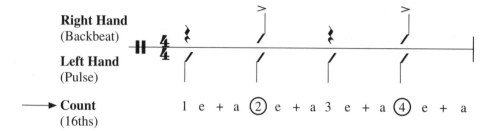

LEARNING "SWEET"

Instead of the backbeat, tap the rhythms of your comping part with your right hand. When you are ready, tap along with the recording. Hook up with the bass, which plays the same rhythm.

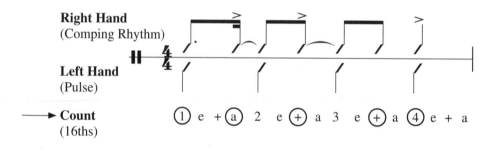

Play your first comping part along with the recording, using the written rhythms. Try to count the sixteenth notes as you play.

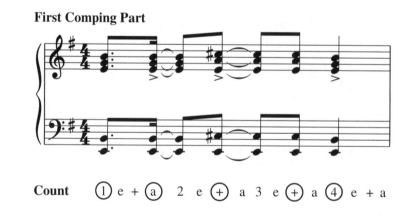

Tap the rhythms of your second comping part, below. When you are ready, tap along with the second part to "Sweet."

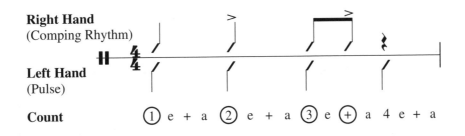

Right Hand
(Comping Rhythm)

Left Hand
(Pulse)

Count

Play your second comping part using the written rhythms. While you play, count the sixteenths, and hook up with the bass and bass drum.

Second Comping Part

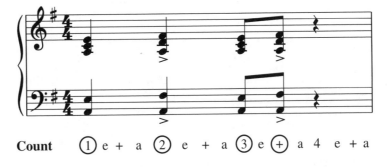

Count

LESSON 3
IMPROVISATION

Improvisation is the invention of a solo. When you improvise, you tell the story of what you think about the tune, and what it means to you. Though an improvised solo may seem spontaneous to the audience, there is a lot of preparation that comes before a musician plays it. There are two things you must know before you start improvising: when you should play, and what notes will sound good.

FORM AND ARRANGEMENT

When you are preparing to improvise on a tune, start by learning how it is organized. This will let you know when you should to start improvising and where the chords change.

LISTEN **1** PLAY

Listen to "Sweet" and follow the saxophone. After an introduction, the sax plays the melody. Then, it improvises a solo. Finally, it plays the melody again.

During the improvised solo, you can still feel the written melody. That's because the improvisation follows the same chords as the written melody. This repeating chord pattern is the same throughout the entire tune, and is called the song's *form*—its plan or structure.

A common way to show this organization is with a *chord chart*. Chord charts don't show rhythm or pitch, just measures and chord symbols. The slash marks (/ / / /) mean "play in time."

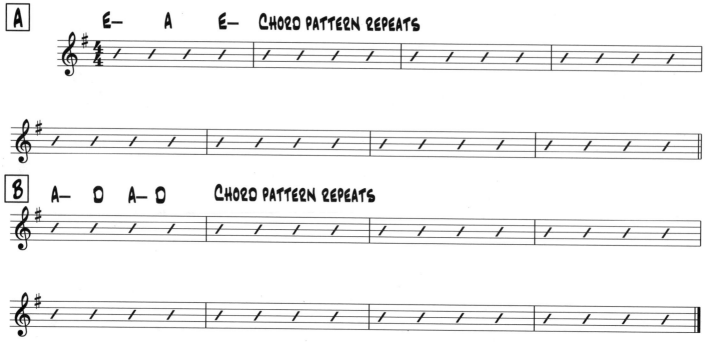

The chord chart makes it easy to see that the form of "Sweet" is sixteen measures long. It has two primary musical ideas: the first eight measures present the first idea (Idea "A"), with the E– A E– patterns. The second eight measures present the second idea (Idea "B"), with the A– D A– D patterns. This form can be described simply as "AB" or "AB form." These letters help us remember the form, freeing us from having to read while we're performing.

One complete repetition of this form is called a *chorus*. A chorus can feature the written melody, in which case it is called the *head*, or it can feature just the chord structure, supporting an improvisation. (The word *chorus* is also used to mean a song section that is alternated with varying verses. In this book, however, the word "chorus" is only used to mean "once through the form.")

ARRANGING "SWEET"

Your band can choose how many choruses you want to play, and create your own *arrangement* of "Sweet." The number of choruses depends on how many players will improvise when you perform the tune. On the recorded performance of "Sweet," only one player solos (the sax), playing for two choruses. Often, several members of the band will take turns playing choruses of improvised solos. A solo can be one or two choruses, or even more.

On the recording, the same basic arrangement is used for all the tunes: the head, an improvised sax solo, and then the head again. There are often short introductions and endings as well. This is the arrangement for "Sweet" played on the recording:

When you play "Sweet" with your band, you can play your own arrangement, adding extra solo choruses, different endings, or other changes.

IDEAS FOR IMPROVISING

When you improvise, some notes will sound better than others. There are many ways to find notes that will sound good. You can use the notes from the tune's melody, you can use notes from the chords, and you can use notes from scales that match the tune. Eventually, this becomes intuitive, and you can just follow your ear.

Pentatonic Scales

The saxophone soloist on this recording of "Sweet" built much of his solo using notes from a *pentatonic scale*. Pentatonic scales are among the simplest and most versatile types of scales in all of music. All pentatonic scales have five notes. There are two common types of pentatonic scales. For "Sweet," the soloist used the *minor pentatonic scale* built on E. This scale works well here because the tune is in E minor.

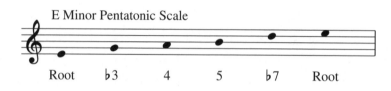

The magic of the minor pentatonic scale is that nearly any series or combination of its notes sounds musically pleasing. It is easy to improvise pentatonic *licks* (short melodic figures or phrases) that sound good.

E Pentatonic Practice

Play this pentatonic melody and chords along with "Sweet."

CALL AND RESPONSE

Echo

Listen to each phrase, and then play it back, echoing it exactly. Each 2-bar phrase comes from the E minor pentatonic scale. Play just the melody, using one hand. Follow the form and try to capture each phrase's rhythms. Slashes ("/") in measures marked "play" mean that you should play during those measures. Listen carefully, and hook up with the groove.

Keep practicing that track until you can echo all phrases perfectly. Then do the same thing for the phrases on this next track.

LISTEN **8** PLAY

Answer

LISTEN **7,8** PLAY

Play the same two tracks again. This time, instead of echoing the phrases exactly, answer them with your own improvised phrases. Imitate the sound and rhythmic feel of the phrases you hear, and only use notes of the E minor pentatonic scale.

Write out some of your own 2-measure phrases, like the ones you have been playing. Don't worry about perfecting your notation; just sketch out your ideas. This will help you remember them when you are improvising.

Create a one-chorus solo using any techniques you have learned. Memorize your solo and practice it along with the recording.

PLAY IN A BAND TIP

When playing in a band, listen to the other players' parts and try to create a musical conversation. This makes playing much more fun, and more musical too. When you are improvising a solo, listen to what the other instruments are playing. They will suggest many ideas that you can use in your solo, and you will inspire each other.

LESSON 4
READING

When you play in a band, sometimes you will get a keyboard part for the tune that shows exactly what you should play. Other times, you will get a lead sheet, giving you more freedom to create your own part. You should be able to play from either one.

KEYBOARD PART

On the next page is the written part to "Sweet." Above your part is a smaller staff that shows the melody and chord symbols. Some keyboard parts show the melody, but often they do not.

INTRO   Introduction. The written part begins with an introduction, which is made up of four measures of the B section.

HARD ROCK   Style indication. This tune is hard rock, and you should play it in that style: strong beat, sixteenth-note feel, and other elements typical of that hard-edged sound.

♩ = 86   Metronome marking. This tells you how fast you should play this tune. If you have a metronome, set it to 86, and play "Sweet" at that tempo.

‖: :‖   Repeat signs. Play the music between these signs twice (or more).

[A]   Rehearsal letter. These are different than form letters, which you saw in lesson 3. These letters help you when you are practicing with other musicians because everyone's parts have the same letters marked at the same places.

[A9]   Rehearsal letter with measure number. These mark different areas within a chorus. Again, this can be helpful during rehearsals.

AFTER SOLOS, REPEAT TO ENDING
     When the soloists are finished, play the head one more time, and then proceed to the measures marked "Ending."

ENDING   A final section that is added to the form. End the tune with these measures.

Play along with the recording of "Sweet," following the notated keyboard part exactly. This part is typical of a comping part that you might create for "Sweet."

Sweet
Keyboard Part

By Matt Marvuglio

LEAD SHEET

Lead sheets present the chords and melody, written in treble clef. Lead sheets give you more interpretive free-dom than full keyboard parts do. Notice that there is no written introduction on this lead sheet. The introduc-tion you hear in the recording is an interpretation of the lead sheet by that band. Your band should create your own unique arrangement.

Play "Sweet" along with the recording, and follow the lead sheet, comping with the chords you learned earlier. Improvise slight variations in the comping rhythm.

SWEET

BY MATT MARVUGLIO

"HARD ROCK" ♩ = 86

PLAY IN A BAND TIP

While you play, follow the lead sheet. It will help you keep your place in the form.

CHAPTER I
DAILY PRACTICE ROUTINE

TECHNIQUE/THEORY: INVERSIONS

There are many ways to play a chord. Pitches can be rearranged, played in different orders and octaves. When a chord tone other than the root appears as the lowest note, the chord is *inverted*. For a triad, two inversions are possible. The example below shows E minor, played in *root position* (the root is the lowest note), and then followed by its two inversions:

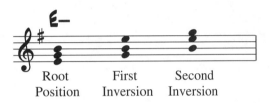

Root Position   First Inversion   Second Inversion

If the third (G) of the chord is the lowest note, then the triad is in *first inversion*. If the fifth (B) is the lowest note, it is in *second inversion*. The inversions you choose will depend on the other instruments in your band, and on the sound you want for the tune.

Here are all the inversions for the chords used in "Sweet."

Practice these inversions in different octaves. Work them into your comping patterns.

PRACTICE TIP

Think of chords and inversions as words in your musical vocabulary. When you learned to talk, you practiced using words by saying them over and over, using them in different ways. When you learn to play music, practice using chords by playing them. As you master how to put them together meaningfully, you may even use them in humorous ways. That's great! Just enjoy finding new ways to play each chord.

Practice the following chord exercise along with the recording (first with each hand separately, and then with both together). Become familiar with the sound of each chord and each inversion. Try different inversions when creating your own comping part to "Sweet."

LEARNING THE GROOVE

Tap the upper rhythms with your right hand, keeping a steady pulse with your left hand. Practice them one line at a time. When you are ready, tap along along with "Sweet."

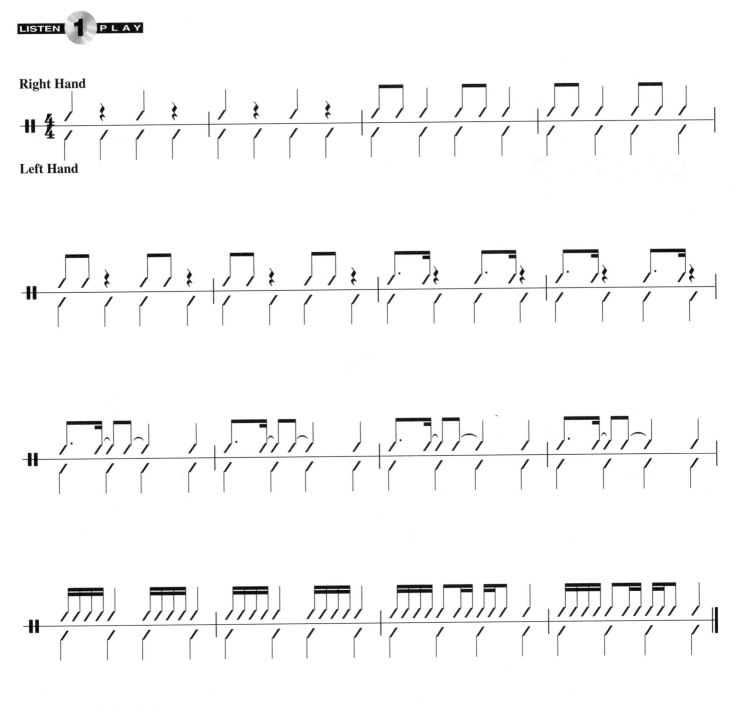

CHALLENGE

Hook up with the recording again, and tap the above rhythms in a random order of your own improvisation.

MEMORIZE

Memorizing the licks and melodies from these exercises will help you play the tune, especially when you improvise. What you practice helps you when you perform. But performing is the best practice, so get together with other musicians and learn these tunes with your own band.

Memorize the comping part to "Sweet." Also memorize the lead sheet. The "Summary" shows everything that you need in order to play "Sweet" from a lead sheet. Memorizing it will help you memorize the tune.

PRACTICE TIP

Write out a chord chart for "Sweet" by memory. This is a good way to help memorize tunes, and you can do it anywhere or anytime. Don't worry about making it neat; just sketch out the measures and the chords, and think about solo ideas you might play over them.

SUMMARY

FORM	ARRANGEMENT	HARMONY	SCALE
16-BAR AB	INTRO: 4 M.		
(1 CHORUS = 16 BARS)	1 CHORUS MELODY		
A: 8 M.	2 CHORUS SOLO		E MINOR PENTATONIC
B: 8 M.	1 CHORUS MELODY		
	END: 2 M.		

PLAY "SWEET" WITH YOUR OWN BAND!

"Do It Now" is a *blues* tune. Blues began in the late 1800s, and it has had a profound influence on American music styles, including rock, jazz, and soul. To hear more blues, listen to artists such as B.B. King, the Blues Brothers, Robben Ford, Bonnie Raitt, James Cotton, Albert King, and Paul Butterfield.

LESSON 5
TECHNIQUE/THEORY

Listen to "Do It Now," and then play along with the recording. Try to match the keyboard part. In this tune, you will play three comping patterns:

First Part   **Second Part**   **Third Part**

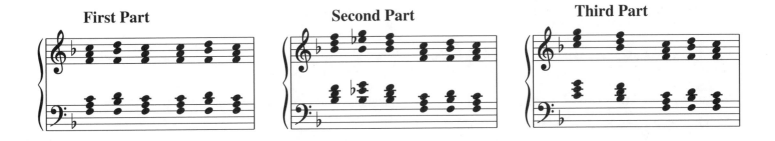

CHORDS: BLUES PROGRESSION

In blues tunes, such as "Do It Now," the basic chords are I, IV, and V. These chord numbers come from the major scale. Here is the F major scale and the number matching each note, or each *scale degree.*

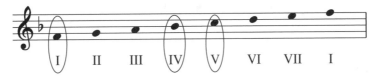

Here are the blues triads built on I, IV, and V. In the key of F, these chords are **F**, **B♭**, and **C**.

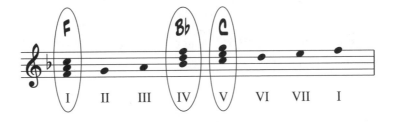

Listen to "Do It Now" and follow the bass, which plays the chord roots. Notice where the chords change. The basic blues progression uses the I, IV, and V chords in this order:

LISTEN **9** PLAY

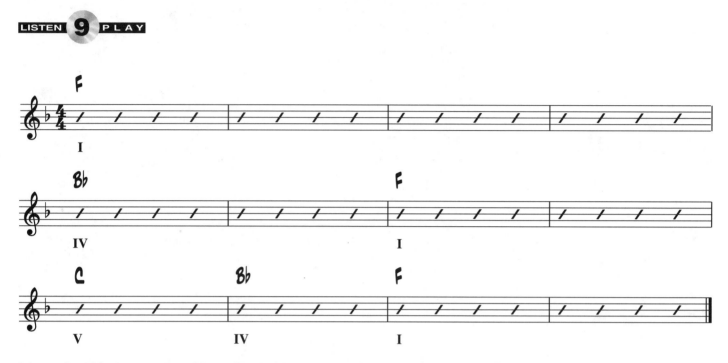

Memorize this progression. You will see it many times, in many forms of music besides blues.

BLUES COMPING PATTERNS

Notice that the keyboard plays two different chords over each root. For example, in the first comping pattern, the chords are notated like this:

But the keyboard part actually plays these chords:

On the recording, the keyboard player created a part by adding the IV chord (B♭), and then returning to the written I chord, F. Mixing in a IV chord when the song only calls for a I chord is common in blues. Choosing the right inversions makes the chord changes sound smooth. In this case, the B♭ chord is in second inversion.

Using the chord a fourth above the written chord will make your blues keyboard parts sound authentic. It will also add a bluesy edge to a rock or jazz tune.

CHORD SYMBOLS: SEVENTH CHORDS

Chord symbols also use numbers to describe extra pitches added to the basic triads, though they use regular numbers (1, 4, 5), rather than Roman numerals (I, IV, V). For example, you may see a chord symbol that looks like this:

FMAJ7

The "maj7" means that you should add the seventh scale degree of the F major scale ("maj" stands for "major"). When you see this symbol, play the notes of this chord:

In blues, and other styles, it is common to use chords that include the ♭7. It is often called the *dominant seventh chord*, and looks like this:

F7

This means that you should add the ♭7 of the F major scale—an E♭. You would play this:

Here are the seventh chords used in "Do It Now." They are all dominant seventh chords.

You can use seventh chords in your own comping part. For example, in this tune, instead of just returning to a simple **F** chord after the **B♭**, as you did in the first phrase, you could go to an **F7**, and add an **E♭** to the chord:

You could do it again from the IV chord (**B♭**):

These dominant seventh chord patterns are common in blues and other styles.

LESSON 6
LEARNING THE GROOVE

HOOKING UP TO A BLUES SHUFFLE

Listen to "Do It Now." This groove has its roots in traditional r&b, gospel, and jazz. The feel is often called a *12/8 shuffle* because of the twelve eighth notes in each bar. (The drums play these on the ride cymbal or hi-hat.)

Tap your left hand on every beat, and count triplets: "1 trip-let 2 trip-let 3 trip-let 4 trip-let." The basic pulse (tap) is on the quarter note. However, each pulse also has an underlying triplet, which divides the beat into three equal parts. Tap the triplets with your right hand.

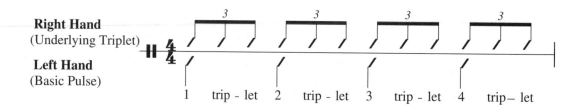

This triplet feel is part of what makes the beat a *shuffle*. While all shuffles don't include triplets on every single beat, the underlying triplet *feel* is always present.

The triplet is a fundamental aspect of all swing and shuffle beats. Understanding and feeling the concept of "subdivisions" (dividing the pulse into smaller rhythms) will help you play many other kinds of grooves.

SWING EIGHTH NOTES

Eighth notes in shuffle grooves are usually played as triplets, even though they are notated as *straight* eighth notes.

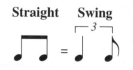

Though these rhythms look different, in some styles, they are played the same. Eighth notes that are played as triplets are called *swing eighth notes*. Swing eighth notes are common in many styles of music, including blues, jazz, and swing. Sometimes, the word "swing," "swing feel," or "shuffle" appears on the lead sheet, telling you how to play eighth notes.

The notated part to "Do It Now" shows eighth notes notated like this:

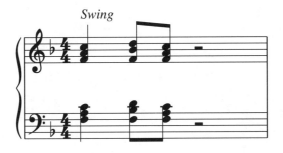

Since it is a shuffle tune, they are played more like this:

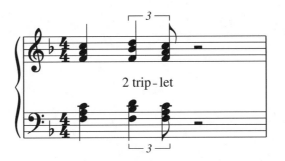

Notating triplets as straight eighths is very common in shuffle grooves.

LESSON 7
IMPROVISATION

LISTEN **9** PLAY

Listen to "Do It Now" and follow the form. Notice that the form is played twice at the head. How many times does it repeat during the improvised solo? Why does the soloist play higher in the second chorus of the improvised solo? Is the keyboard part the same or different during the solo? Why?

FORM AND ARRANGEMENT: 12-BAR BLUES

"Do It Now" is a *12-bar blues*. As you saw in lesson 1, its form is twelve measures long.

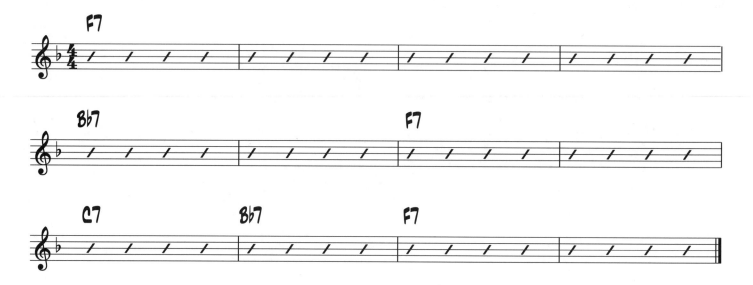

A 12-bar blues has three 4-bar phrases. It is common for the first two phrases in the melody to be similar and the third one to be different. This form is very common in many styles of music, including jazz, rock, and funk.

"Do It Now" begins with the drum playing two beats of triplets. This is called a *pickup*—a short introduction, less than a measure long, that leads to a strong downbeat. The arrangement played on the recording is:

PICKUP	HEAD: 2x	SAX SOLO: 2x	HEAD	ENDING
2 Beats Drums	‖: 1 Chorus = 12 Measures :‖:	1 Chorus = 12 Measures :‖	1 Chorus = 12 Measures ‖	4 Measures ‖

IDEAS FOR IMPROVISING: BLUES SCALE

In chapter 1, you learned to improvise using the minor pentatonic scale.

Here is the F minor pentatonic scale:

The *F blues scale* has just one more note—the flat fifth scale tone (C♭ or B natural):

The blues scale is linked closely to the blues chord progression. Every note of the blues scale will sound good over every chord in the blues progression, though it has more tension than the minor pentatonic scale does. This tension makes melodies interesting, and blues scales are very popular among improvisers.

Play the F blues scale slowly over all three roots of the blues progression. Listen to how each note of this scale sounds against each of the three roots.

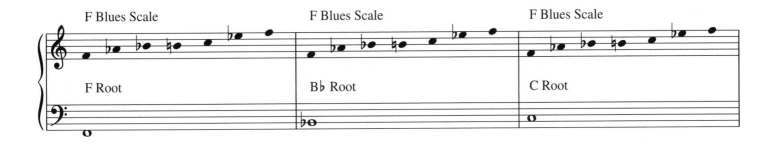

Practice the F blues scale over the chords to "Do It Now," using the fingerings shown. When you are ready, play this exercise along with the recording.

CHALLENGE

Play the F blues scale up and down, over two or three octaves. Play it with both hands. This will help you have better control over the notes of the scale while you improvise.

CALL AND RESPONSE

1. Echo each phrase, exactly as you hear it.
2. Improvise an answer to each phrase. Imitate the sound and rhythmic feel of the phrase you hear, and use notes from the F blues scale.

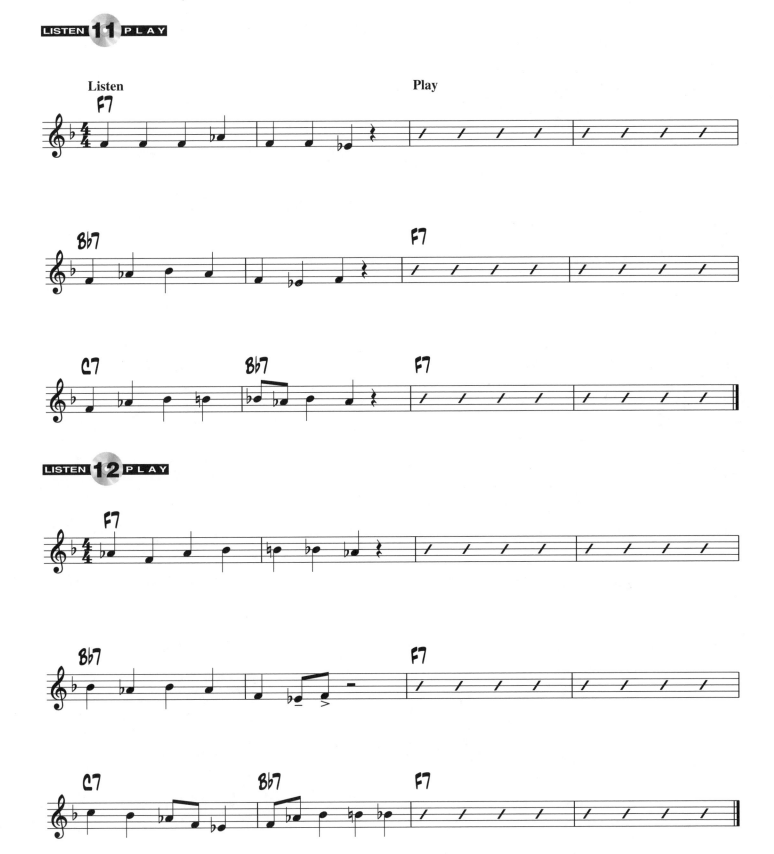

Write out a few of your own ideas. Use notes from the F blues scale.

LISTEN 10 PLAY

Create a one-chorus solo using any techniques you have learned. Memorize your solo and practice it along with the recording.

LESSON 8
READING

KEYBOARD PART

This *chart* (written part) uses symbols and instructions that direct you to skip around the pages. When you get the hang of these symbols, you will see that they help reduce the number of written measures and make the chart easier to read quickly, at a glance. Sometimes, these directions are called the chart's *road map*.

2 BEATS DRUMS Pickup. Short introduction (less than a measure).

𝄋 Sign. Later, there will be a direction (D.S., or "from the sign") telling you to jump to this symbol from another location in the music.

⊕ Coda symbol. "Coda" is another word for "ending." On the last chorus, skip from the first coda symbol to the second coda symbol (at the end of the piece). This symbol may also have the words "To Coda," or other directions (such as "last time only"). Often, you will just see the coda symbol by itself.

D.S. AL ⊕ From the sign (𝄋), and take the coda. Jump back to the sign (first measure, after the pickup), and play from there. When you reach the first coda symbol, skip ahead to the next coda symbol (at the end).

AFTER SOLOS When all solo choruses are finished, follow this direction.

B Different choruses may be marked with different letters. In this tune, the head is marked "A," and the improvisation choruses are marked "B."

SOLO Solo chorus. Play this part when other musicians in the band improvise. When you play this tune with your own band, you might repeat this section several times, depending on how many people solo. When you solo, then obviously, you won't play this written part.

Play "Do It Now" along with the recording. Follow the keyboard part exactly as it is written. It uses the comping patterns you have been playing throughout this chapter.

LISTEN 10 PLAY

Do It Now

Keyboard Part

By Matt Marvuglio

B SOLOS

F7

Bb7   F7

After solos, D.S. al ⊕

C7   Bb7   F7

CODA ⊕

C7   Bb7   F7

LEAD SHEET

Play "Do It Now" and follow the lead sheet. Play your own comping part.

CHAPTER II
DAILY PRACTICE ROUTINE

BLUES COMPING PATTERNS

Practice these I-IV-I patterns, which begin on different inversions. Each time, the IV-chord inversion chosen is the one whose notes are closest to the original chord.

INVERSIONS

In chapter 1, you learned that triads have two possible inversions. Seventh chords have three possible inversions. *Third inversion* is when the seventh is the lowest note.

Third Inversion

Here are the inversions for the "Do It Now" chords. Play each inversion in several octaves. Notice how their sound changes in the different registers.

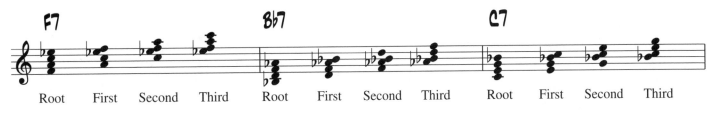

The following exercise covers all the inversions of the "Do It Now" chords. Practice the chords in both right and left hands. Use some of these inversions when you create your own comping part to "Do It Now."

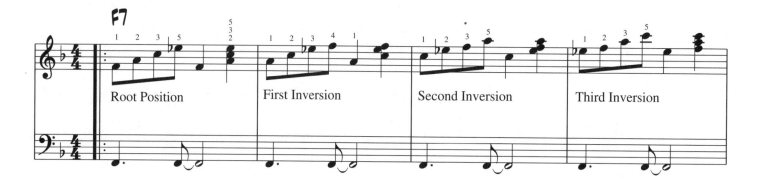

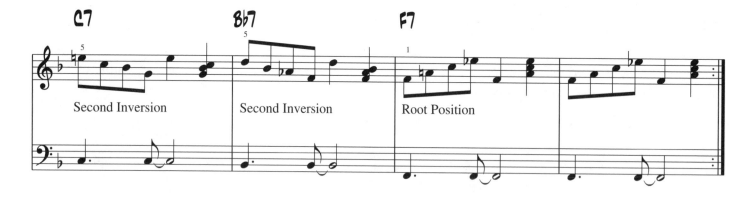

Using inversions from the previous exercise, create a comping part using the rhythms below. Swing your eighths, and practice it along with the recording.

Comping Rhythms 1

Comping Rhythms 2

CHALLENGE

Create a comping part to "Do It Now" using your own rhythms. Play it along with the recording.

CALL AND RESPONSE

1. Echo each phrase, exactly as you hear it.
2. Improvise an answer to each phrase. Imitate the sound and rhythmic feel of the phrase you hear, and use the notes from the F blues scale.

Write out a few of your own ideas. Use notes of the F blues scale.

Create a comping part and a solo using any techniques you have learned. Memorize your part, and then play through the tune with the recording as if you were performing it live. Keep your place in the form, and don't stop, whatever happens.

> ### PERFORMANCE TIP
>
> If you make a mistake or get lost, keep your composure, and pretend that everything is going fine. Listen to the other instruments, hear what chords they are playing, and find your way back into the form. You can even practice getting lost and then finding your place. Start the recording at a random point within the track, and then follow your ear.

SUMMARY

FORM	ARRANGEMENT	HARMONY	SCALE
12-BAR BLUES (1 CHORUS = 12 BARS)	PICKUP: 2 BEATS DRUMS 2 CHORUS MELODY 2 CHORUS SOLO 1 CHORUS MELODY END: 4 M.	F7 Bb7 C7	F BLUES

PLAY "DO IT NOW" WITH YOUR OWN BAND!

"I Just Wanna Be With You" is a *blues swing*. *Swing* is a dance-oriented, big-band style from the 1930s. To hear more swing, listen to artists such as Count Basie, Benny Goodman, the Squirrel Nut Zippers, Diana Krall, Branford Marsalis, Kevin Eubanks, Joanne Brackeen, Cherry Poppin' Daddies, and Big Bad Voodoo Daddy.

LESSON 9
TECHNIQUE/THEORY

Listen to "I Just Wanna Be With You," and then play along with the recording. Try to match the keyboard part. In this tune, you will play three comping patterns. Notice that the first pattern returns after the third pattern.

LISTEN **15** PLAY

First Comping Pattern   **Second Comping Pattern**   **Third Comping Pattern**

BLUES SWING COMPING PATTERNS

"I Just Wanna Be With You" is also a blues tune. The chords follow the same blues pattern, using the I, IV, and V chords as "Do It Now." The difference is that this tune is based on minor chords.

This tune also uses the same I–IV–I chord comping patterns as "Do It Now." In these comping patterns, the I chords are all minor triads, but the IVs are all major. Minor and major chords in the same pattern give minor-blues a unique sound.

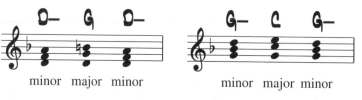

42

INVERSIONS FOR COMPING PATTERNS

In the first comping pattern, there are two chords: D minor and G major. Here are the inversions for both chords.

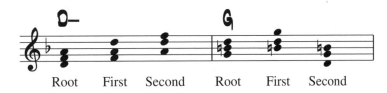

Root   First   Second   Root   First   Second

In the comping pattern, the I chord (D–) is in first inversion. The IV chord (G) is in root position.

First   Root

We use different inversions for the two chords so that the comping pattern sounds smooth. If both chords were in root position, it would sound choppy.

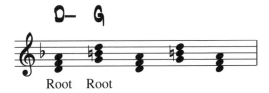

Root   Root

The way that one chord moves to another is called *voice leading*. Using the right inversions leads to smoother voice leading and better comping parts. Smooth voice leading helps the keyboard part blend into the groove. In the actual comping pattern, notice that the top note "D" appears in both chords and stays in the same position. The other notes all move by only a step. We say that such a part "has smooth voice leading" or simply "is voice led." When you move to a new chord, generally you should move each voice as little as possible, unless you are trying to get a disjointed effect.

LESSON 10
LEARNING THE GROOVE

HOOKING UP TO SWING

LISTEN **15** PLAY

Listen to "I Just Wanna Be With You" and focus on the cymbals. This tune is a shuffle, like "Do It Now." There is a triplet feel under each beat. The main difference is that in this tune, the middle triplet of each beat is left out. This is common in swing.

Shuffle ("Do It Now")	**Swing Shuffle** ("I Just Wanna...")

This syncopated "push-pull" feel is basic to jazz and r&b. Sometimes this feel is called a "double shuffle" because the drummer plays the same rhythm with both hands. In swing, the bass player usually plays a "walking" quarter-note bass line.

Notice how the sax interprets the ♪♪ of the melody. The eighth notes are uneven, or "bounced." Try to sing or play along with the sax. This will help you get into the swing feel.

Learning "I Just Wanna Be With You"

Listen carefully to the rhythms from the melody indicated below. These same rhythms are picked up by the keyboard comping part. After listening to the melody, play along with the comping rhythm. Imitate the rhythmic feel that the sax uses in rhythms 1 and 2.

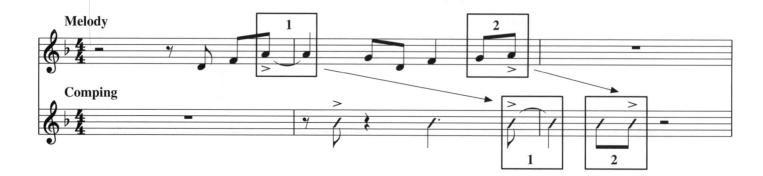

Let's break down the comping rhythm into two rhythms. Tap quarter notes with your foot. With your hand, tap this rhythm.

The first measure of the comping rhythm is the same except that the first attack is *delayed*.

Now, look at the second measure of the comping part. Notice that the third attack is *anticipated*. Tap quarter notes with your foot, and the comping rhythm with your hand.

One more rhythm will complete this comping pattern. Start with the comping rhythm above. Then, anticipate the first attack.

When you are comfortable playing these rhythms, you will be ready to find this tune's groove.

LESSON 11
IMPROVISATION

FORM AND ARRANGEMENT

Listen to "I Just Wanna Be With You" and follow the form. This tune is another 12-bar blues. The form of each chorus is twelve measures long and divided into three phrases, just like "Do It Now."

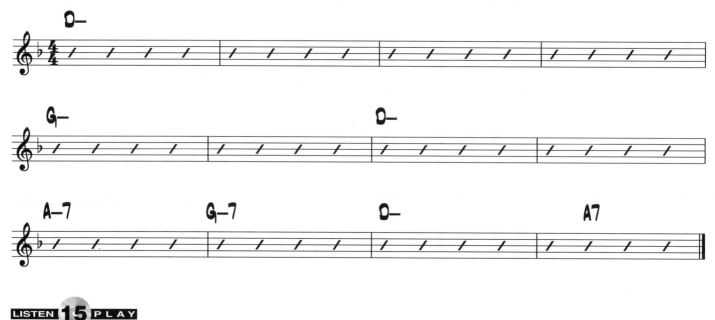

LISTEN 15 PLAY

Listen to "I Just Wanna Be With You" and follow the arrangement. Is there an introduction or ending? What part of the form did these added sections come from?

This is the arrangement used on the recording:

INTRO	HEAD: 2x	SAX SOLO: 2x	HEAD	ENDING
4 MEASURES	1 CHORUS = 12 MEASURES	1 CHORUS = 12 MEASURES	1 CHORUS = 12 MEASURES	8 MEASURES

The intro and ending come from the form's last four measures. On the recording, the band chose to play the ending twice. This kind of repeated ending is called a *tag ending*.

PERFORMANCE TIP

Sometimes, a band may decide to "tag a tune" (play a tag ending) several times, building energy with each repetition. If things are going well and everyone is in the mood, a band may even make an ending longer than the rest of the tune. This is a place where people really let loose and have fun playing. When you listen to music, pay attention to what a band is doing at the end of a tune.

Though the soloist on the recording favors the D minor pentatonic scale, the *D blues* scale will also work well for this tune. It has one additional note—the A♭:

Play the D blues scale with your right hand, up and down within the octave, while you play the chords to "I Just Wanna Be With You" with your left hand. Follow the song form.

LISTEN **16** PLAY

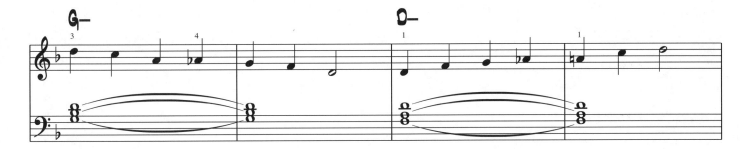

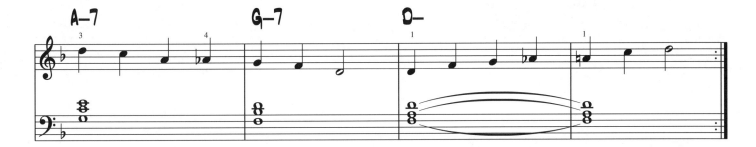

CALL AND RESPONSE

1. Echo each phrase, exactly as you hear it.
2. Improvise an answer to each phrase. Imitate the sound and rhythmic feel of the phrase you hear, and use the notes from the D blues scale.

Write out a few of your own ideas. Use the D blues scale.

Create a one-chorus solo using any techniques you have learned. Memorize your solo and practice it along with the recording.

LESSON 12
READING

KEYBOARD PART

Play "I Just Wanna Be With You" while reading from the written keyboard part. Play it as written.

$\frac{2}{\text{⫻}}$ Two-measure repeat. Repeat the previously-notated two measures.

LISTEN **16** PLAY

I Just Wanna Be With You

Keyboard Part

By Matt Marvuglio

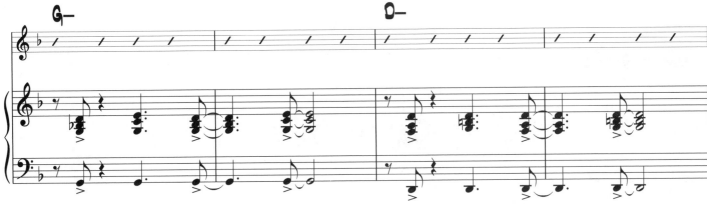

LEAD SHEET

Play "I Just Wanna Be With You" from the lead sheet, using your own comping part. There are two new notation items here:

   Break your regular comping rhythm when you see this (last measure) and play this rhythm instead.

INTRO/ENDING   Though this lead sheet doesn't show an introduction or ending, you and your band can create your own. The intro can be just drums, as you saw in "Do It Now," or it can come from the last line of the tune, as it does on the recording. Tag the ending at least three times, repeating the last four measures of the written part.

LISTEN **16** PLAY

I JUST WANNA BE WITH YOU

BY MATT MARVUGLIO

CHAPTER III
DAILY PRACTICE ROUTINE

INVERSION PRACTICE

Practice this inversion exercise along with the recording.

MELODY/COMPING PRACTICE

Practice playing melody against a comping part, first by yourself, and then with the recording.

CHALLENGE

While you play chords in your left hand, improvise with your right hand using the D blues scale.

DRONE EFFECTS

Try these blues licks.

1. Practice the D minor blues scale with an added upper note. Think of the the lower note as the melody and the upper note as a *drone* (sustained) harmony. Practice slowly, up and down the scale, until it feels natural.

2. Now, practice dividing the scale into triplets, adding the drone on the first of each triplet group.

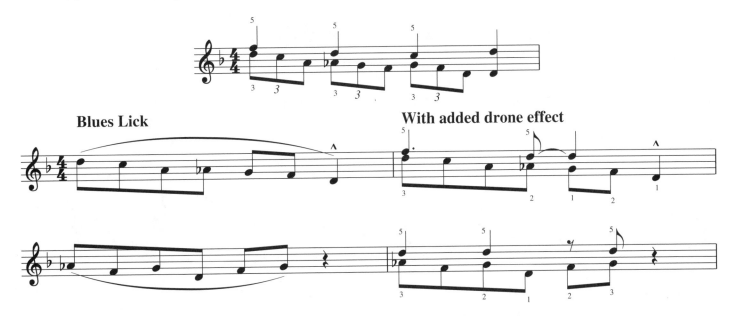

Blues Lick   **With added drone effect**

CHALLENGE

LISTEN **16** PLAY

Create a one-chorus solo that uses the drone effect. Practice it along with the recording.

MEMORIZE

LISTEN **16** PLAY

Create your own comping part and improvised solo to "I Just Wanna Be With You." Practice it along with the recording, and memorize it.

SUMMARY

FORM
12-BAR BLUES
(1 CHORUS = 12 BARS)

ARRANGEMENT
INTRO: 4 M.
2 CHORUS MELODY
2 CHORUS SOLO
1 CHORUS MELODY
END: 6 M.

HARMONY

D— G— G—7 A— A—7 A7

SCALE

D BLUES

PLAY "I JUST WANNA BE WITH YOU" WITH YOUR OWN BAND!

"Leave Me Alone" is a *funk* tune. Funk has its roots in New Orleans street music. It started in the 1960s and is a combination of rock, r&b, Motown, jazz, and blues. Funk has also influenced many rap artists. To hear more funk, listen to artists such as James Brown, Tower of Power, Kool and the Gang, the Yellowjackets, Chaka Khan, Tina Turner, and the Red Hot Chili Peppers.

LESSON 13
TECHNIQUE/THEORY

Listen to "Leave Me Alone," and then play along with the recording. Try to match the keyboard part. In this tune, you will play three comping patterns:

First Comping Pattern

Second Comping Pattern

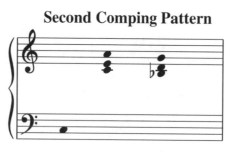

Third Comping Pattern

COMPING IN FUNK

The funk style uses heavy bass lines, and the keyboard part sometimes overlaps with what the bass is playing. In the other tunes you have been playing, your right and left hands have played the same rhythms. In this tune, your right hand will play chords, but often, your left hand will double the bass part.

Listen to "Leave Me Alone" and focus on the keyboard and bass parts. The keyboard generally doubles the bass, though there are a few differences.

LISTEN **19** PLAY

Bass

Keyboard Left Hand

On the first beat, the keyboard plays the octave figure, while the bass holds for a quarter note. On the last three notes, they both play the same rhythm; the keyboard plays the same pitches but the bass changes the riff each time. On the second beat, the right hand hooks up with the bass rhythm, playing chords.

Keyboard Right Hand

As you can see, the keyboard part supports the bass line. The small differences in the two parts make the groove sound more interesting.

LESSON 14
LEARNING THE GROOVE

HOOKING UP TO FUNK

LISTEN **19** PLAY

Listen to "Leave Me Alone." This funk groove has its roots in New Orleans street music—funky march music played on marching instruments (snare drums, bass drums, and so on) still found in the Mardi Gras parades each spring. Many New Orleans artists were important to the development of funk.

Funk rhythms are played with less of a swing feel than blues. There is an underlying sixteenth-note feel, similar to rock. Beats 2 and 4 are often accented, usually by the snare drum.

SYNCOPATION

In the last chapter, you learned to play syncopated eighth notes. In funk, syncopations are often on sixteenth notes. "Leave Me Alone" has a syncopated sixteenth note at the end of the second beat. This note interrupts the regular pulse.

Syncopation

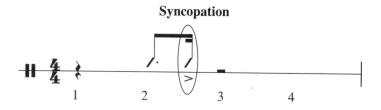

To get the right feel, start by clapping the second note on beat 3.

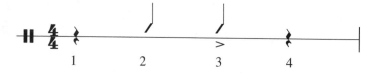

Next, clap the the second note a sixteenth sooner. It comes right before beat 3. This type of syncopation is often called an *anticipation* because it "anticipates" the beat.

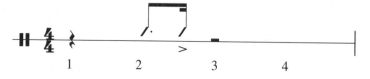

Play your comping part using the written rhythms. Feel the anticipated rhythm.

LESSON 15
IMPROVISATION

FORM AND ARRANGEMENT

Listen to "Leave Me Alone" and follow the form. This funk tune follows the 12-bar blues form.

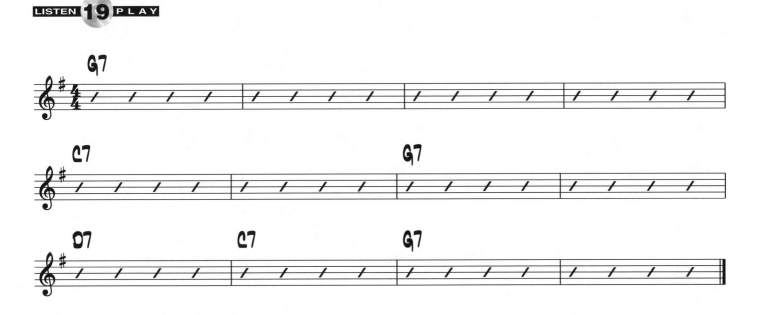

On the recording, the arrangement begins with a 4-measure introduction, featuring the rhythm section playing the groove.

IDEAS FOR IMPROVISING

Scale: G Blues Scale

The G blues scale will work well for this tune:

CALL AND RESPONSE

1. Echo each phrase, exactly as you hear it.
2. Improvise an answer to each phrase. Imitate the sound and rhythmic feel of the phrase you hear, and use the notes from the G blues scale.

Write out a few of your own ideas.

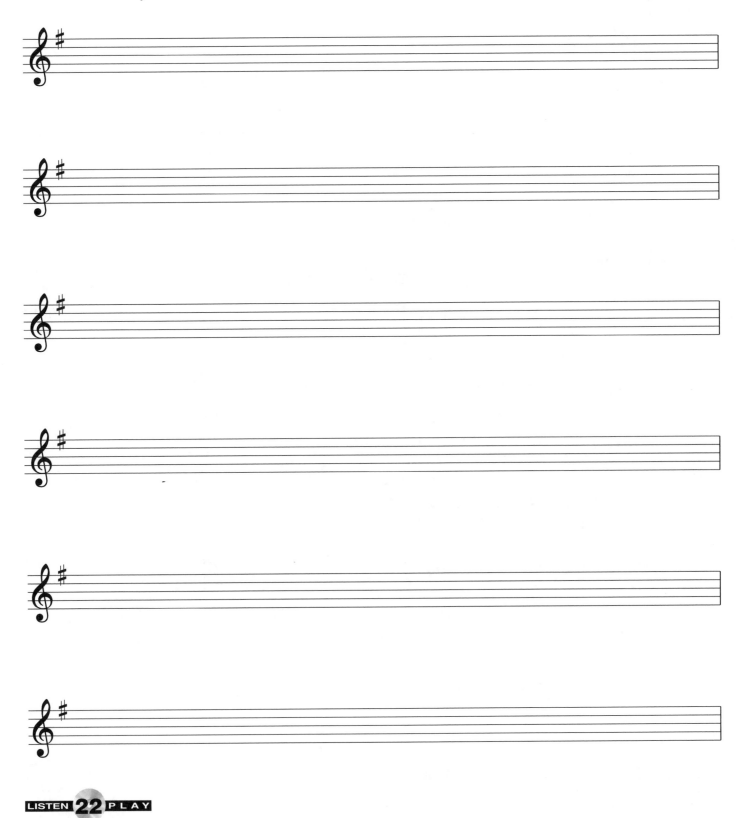

Create a one-chorus solo using any techniques you have learned. Memorize your solo and practice it along with the recording.

LESSON 16
READING

KEYBOARD PART

4 A bar with a number over it means that you should rest for that number of measures. The introduction
here is just bass and drums, so you can sit out. But count along, so you are ready to come in on the
fifth measure.

Play "Leave Me Alone" along with the recording, using the written keyboard part.

LISTEN **22** PLAY

LEAVE ME ALONE
KEYBOARD PART
BY MATT MARVUGLIO

LEAD SHEET

Play "Leave Me Alone" along with the recording, and follow the lead sheet. Play your own comping part.

LEAVE ME ALONE

BY MATT MARVUGLIO

CHAPTER IV
DAILY PRACTICE ROUTINE

INVERSION PRACTICE

Here are all the inversions for the chords used in "Leave Me Alone."

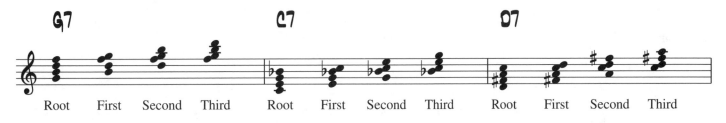

Practice this inversion exercise along with the recording. First play it as written, then switch hands.

HOOKING UP

Practice hooking up with the funk groove's sixteenth-note feel. Tap the quarter-note pulse with your left hand and the upper rhythms with your right hand. Repeat each rhythm until you can play it easily.

CHALLENGE

Play this exercise again, and count "1 e + a, 2 e + a, 3 e + a, 4 e + a" as you tap quarter notes with your left hand. For an added challenge, play and count along with the recording. Try switching hands.

Practice your comping part again, with the recording, playing the rhythms as precisely as possible.

CALL AND RESPONSE

1. Echo each phrase, exactly as you hear it.
2. Improvise an answer to each phrase. Imitate the sound and rhythmic feel of the phrase you hear, and use the notes from the G blues scale.

Listen   **Play**

Write out a few of your own ideas.

Create a one-chorus solo using any techniques you have learned. Memorize your solo and practice it along with the recording.

MEMORIZE

LISTEN **22** PLAY

Create your own comping part and improvised solo to "Leave Me Alone." Practice it along with the recording, and memorize it.

SUMMARY

FORM	ARRANGEMENT	HARMONY	SCALE
12-BAR BLUES (1 CHORUS = 12 BARS)	INTRO: 4 M. 2 CHORUS MELODY 2 CHORUS SOLO 1 CHORUS MELODY	G7 C7 D7	G BLUES

PLAY "LEAVE ME ALONE" WITH YOUR OWN BAND!

"Affordable" is another funk tune, but it is lighter, with more of a feeling of open space. This style is popular with smooth-jazz artists. To hear more light funk, listen to artists such as David Sanborn, Earl Klugh, Walter Beasley, the Rippingtons, Dave Grusin, Kenny G, Bob James, and Anita Baker.

LESSON 17
TECHNIQUE/THEORY

Listen to "Affordable," and then play along with the recording. Try to match the keyboard. This tune has two parts.

First Comping Pattern

Second Comping Pattern

CHORDS: ADDING COLOR TO SEVENTH CHORDS

Keyboardists sometimes add notes to seventh chords to make a comping part more interesting. This is similar to what you saw in the I-IV-I blues pattern—adding a IV chord when only a I chord is indicated on the lead sheet. Two common additions to seventh chords are the 4 and the 9.

Added 4

The first part of "Affordable" is based on the G7 chord.

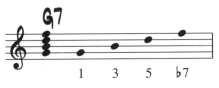

The first comping part uses a common comping pattern for seventh chords: moving to the standard G7 chord from a G7 chord with a 4 (C) instead of a 3 (B). This kind of chord is called a *sus4*. Here is a G7sus4:

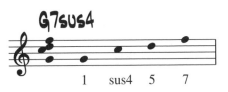

Play the first part to "Affordable," and notice the **G7sus4** moving to a **G7**.

If the lead sheet had "**G7sus4**," instead of "**G7**," the chord would not need to move to the **G7**. The second comping part in "Affordable" is based on a written **C7sus4**. Since sus4 is specified, the part "suspends" the 4 above C (F) over the whole section.

Added 9

It is also common to add the 9 to a comping part. The second comping pattern of "Affordable" is a good example. The written chord symbol is a **C7sus4** chord.

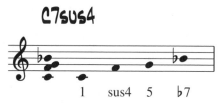

The keyboardist on the recording added a 9 (D) to his comping part to give it more color.

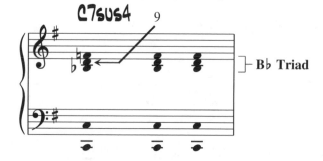

Notice that the upper three notes form a **Bb** major triad. Another way to describe this chord is with the symbol **Bb/C**. This means a **Bb** chord with the note C in the bass. You may see it written either as **Bb/C** or as **C7sus4**, but the notes are the same.

Try adding a sus4 or 9 to your own comping parts. It is a good way to add color to your chords.

LESSON 18
LEARNING THE GROOVE

HOOKING UP TO LIGHT FUNK

LISTEN **25** PLAY

Listen to "Affordable." This groove is built around eighth notes, with some syncopated sixteenths in the B section. Notice that the band hooks up with the bass drum.

To learn this feel, practice counting sixteenths, leaving out the middle two sixteenths of each beat. Count out loud, along with a metronome or click track on the quarter-note pulse.

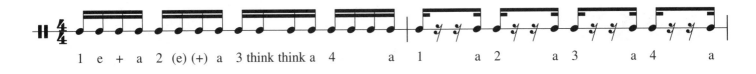

1   e   +   a   2   (e)   (+)   a   3   think   think   a   4   a   1   a   2   a   3   a   4   a

The melody of "Affordable" is mostly made up of long, sustained notes. Listening to the rest of the rhythm section and counting will help you keep your place.

In these exercises, tap the quarter-note pulse with your left hand and eighth notes with your right hand. Remember that the eighth notes are played straight, not with a swing feel. This is a slow tempo so be careful not to rush. Let's start with the second measure of the comping rhythm and compare it to an unsyncopated rhythm:

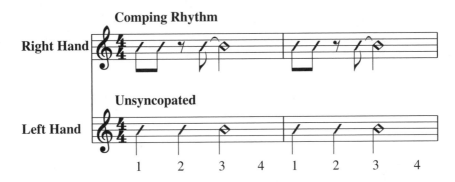

Notice that the second and third attacks are anticipated one half-beat early. Tap quarter notes with your left hand and this comping rhythm with your right hand until you can do it comfortably.

The rhythm of the first measure of the comping pattern is similar except that there is one more attack. Compare this rhythm to four straight quarter notes.

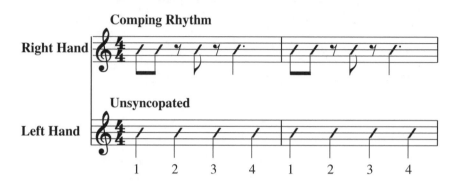

Notice that the second, third, and fourth attacks are all anticipated. Again, tap quarter notes with your left hand and the comping rhythm with your right hand until you can do it comfortably.

PRACTICE TIP

This exercise will help you play syncopations. Tap quarter notes with your left hand and eighth notes with your right hand, as before.

Then tap only the offbeats.

Finally, tap the comping rhythm.

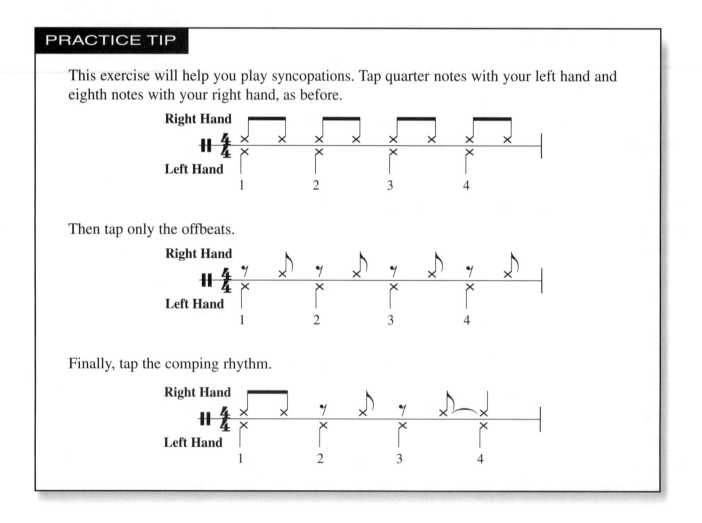

LESSON 19
IMPROVISATION

FORM AND ARRANGEMENT

Listen to "Affordable" and follow the saxophone melody over the 16-bar form.

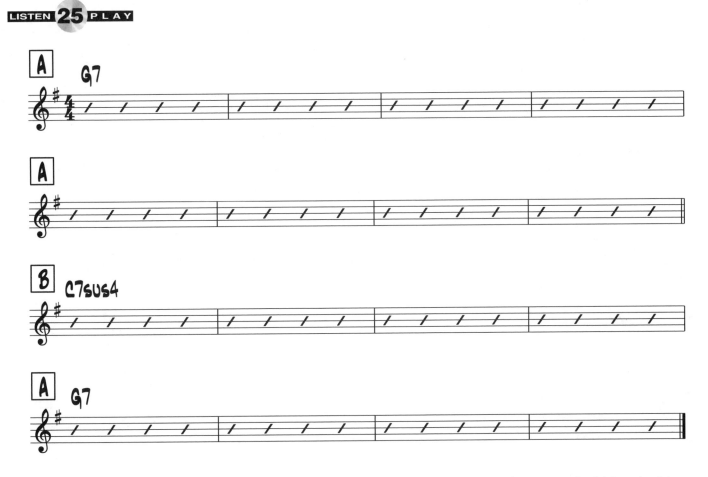

As you have already seen from practicing the comping patterns, there are two primary musical ideas in this tune. The sax plays contrasting melodies over them. Idea A is very sparse. It lasts for eight measures, with two phrases of sax melody. Idea B is in a more regular rhythm. It lasts for four measures. Then Idea A returns for four measures. This form can be described simply as "AABA."

Listen to the whole tune. Sing the melody while the saxophone plays the solo, and keep your place in the form. What is the arrangement on the recording? Is there an introduction or ending? Check your answer against the summary at the end of this chapter.

IDEAS FOR IMPROVISING

Scale

The G major pentatonic scale will work well for the A section of this tune:

The G minor pentatonic scale will work well for the B section of this tune:

CALL AND RESPONSE

1. Echo each phrase, exactly as you hear it.
2. Improvise an answer to each phrase. Imitate the sound and rhythmic feel of the phrase you hear, and use the notes from the G pentatonic scales.

Listen

Play

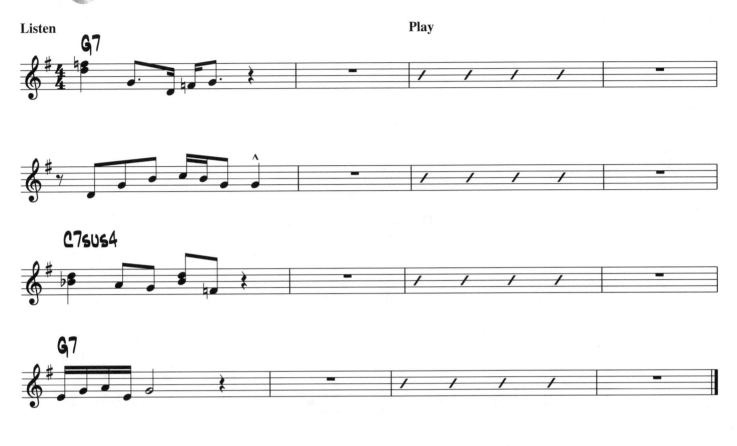

Write out a few of your own ideas. Use the G pentatonic scales.

Create a one-chorus solo using any techniques you have learned. Memorize your solo and practice it along with the recording.

KEYBOARD PART

Play "Affordable" along with the recording. Use the written keyboard part. Notice the use of bass clef in the right hand. This reduces the need for ledger lines.

AFFORDABLE

Keyboard Part

By Matt Marvuglio

LEAD SHEET

Play "Affordable" along with the recording, and follow the lead sheet. Create your own comping part.

LISTEN **28** PLAY

AFFORDABLE

BY MATT MARVUGLIO

CHAPTER V
DAILY PRACTICE ROUTINE

TECHNIQUE/THEORY: INVERSION PRACTICE

Practice the inversions of the **G7**, **G7sus4**, and **C7sus4** chords:

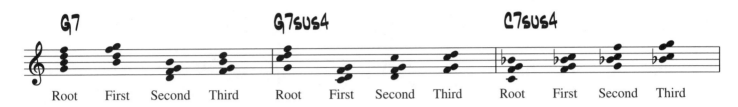

Practice the inversions of the chords used in "Affordable."

MIXOLYDIAN SCALES

Another scale you can use to improvise on this tune is the Mixolydian scale. Use the G Mixolydian scale during the "A" sections of "Affordable," over the **G7** chords:

Use the C Mixolydian scale during the "B" section, over the **C7sus4** chords.

Play the following exercise, and listen carefully to the sound and character of each note. The left-hand "bass and chord" part establishes the harmony. Over the harmony, the scale is played as a melody. Try starting on different steps of the Mixolydian scales over each accompaniment.

HARMONIZING THE MELODY

Using the notes of G Mixolydian, complete a second inversion triad under each scale note, using only scale notes. This is a common technique keyboard players use to harmonize melodies in funk and other styles.

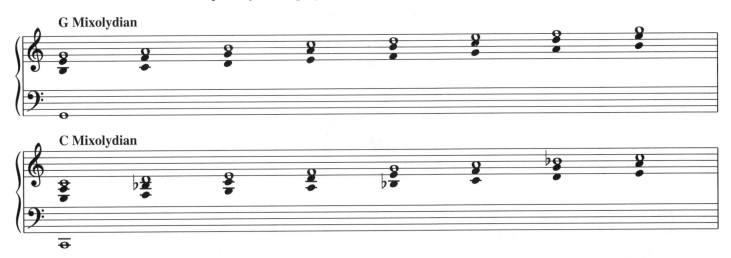

Practice playing the melody of "Affordable," harmonizing each melody note using the above technique. Play the scale roots with your left hand.

MEMORIZE

Create your own comping part and improvised solo to "Affordable." Practice it along with the recording, and memorize it.

SUMMARY

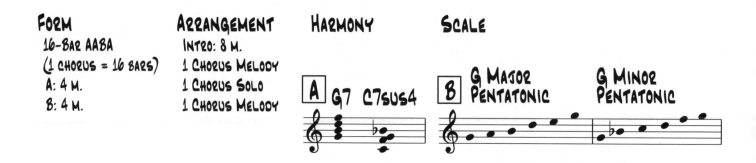

FORM
16-BAR AABA
(1 CHORUS = 16 BARS)
A: 4 M.
B: 4 M.

ARRANGEMENT
INTRO: 8 M.
1 CHORUS MELODY
1 CHORUS SOLO
1 CHORUS MELODY

HARMONY
A | G7 C7SUS4

SCALE
B | G MAJOR PENTATONIC   G MINOR PENTATONIC

PLAY "AFFORDABLE" WITH YOUR OWN BAND!

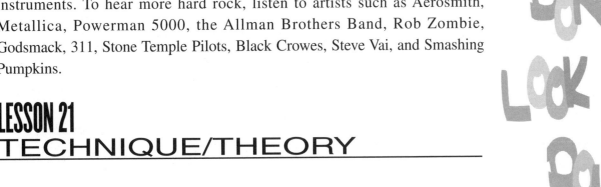

"Don't Look Down" is a *hard rock* tune. Hard rock first appeared in the late 1960s. It has characteristic heavy bass, long, drawn-out chords, and amplified instruments. To hear more hard rock, listen to artists such as Aerosmith, Metallica, Powerman 5000, the Allman Brothers Band, Rob Zombie, Godsmack, 311, Stone Temple Pilots, Black Crowes, Steve Vai, and Smashing Pumpkins.

LESSON 21
TECHNIQUE/THEORY

Listen to "Don't Look Down," and then play along with the recording. Try to match the keyboard part. This tune has two parts.

LISTEN 29 PLAY

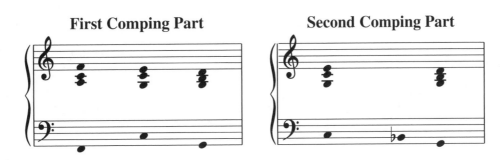

First Comping Part   Second Comping Part

PAD COMPING

The chords are long and sustained in this tune. This way of playing chords is called *pad comping*. It is most effective with organs and electronic keyboards set to sounds that hold without fading, such as string and organ sounds.

Pad comping works well especially when the other instruments are playing busier parts. "Don't Look Down" has a busy bass line and rock drum beat, as well as an active melody. The keyboard's pad comping part holds it all together:

For variety, you may wish to double the bass line with your left hand:

LESSON 22
LEARNING THE GROOVE

HOOKING UP TO HARD ROCK

Listen to "Don't Look Down." This tune has a standard rock/metal groove. It is a heavy feel, with very simple drum and bass parts. These parts must be simple because they are intended to be played in large arenas, where echoes would make busier parts sound muddy. It's a case of "less is more."

Eighth notes are played straight, not with a swing feel. The bass drum plays on beats 1 and 3, which is typical of rock drum beats.

Listen to a few choruses of "Don't Look Down." Find the pulse and clap on the backbeat, along with the snare drum.

```
              >           >
   1     2     3     4
```

Tap the quarter-note pulse with your left hand, tap the backbeat with your right hand, and count the sixteenths. When you are ready, do this along with the recording.

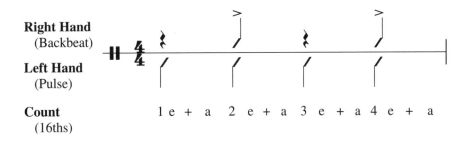

LEARNING "DON'T LOOK DOWN"

LISTEN **30** PLAY

"Don't Look Down" has two different parts with two different rhythmic feels. In the first part, the keyboard plays the pad comping chords. Since there is just one attack on the downbeat of each measure, these are easy to play.

Listen to the first part of "Don't Look Down." Feel the sixteenth-note subdivision even when you play simple parts like this, especially if you plan to improvise a solo, where you might decide to use faster rhythms.

The second part has a syncopation. Tap the comping rhythms to the second part of "Don't Look Down." Accent the syncopated note.

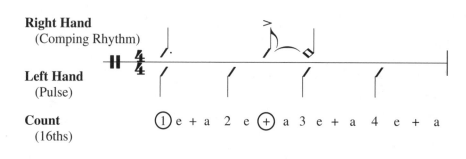

Play the second written comping part. While you play, count the sixteenths and hook up with the groove.

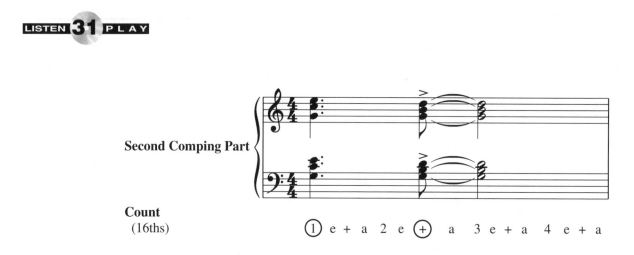

LESSON 23
IMPROVISATION

FORM AND ARRANGEMENT

Listen to the recording and try to figure out the form and arrangement by ear. How long does each section of the form last? Is there an introduction or ending? For how many measures or beats does each chord last? Write down as much information as you can. Check your answers against the keyboard part in the next lesson.

This tune has a 20-bar AB form. Part A has an active riff that builds a lot of tension. It lasts for sixteen measures. Part B is less active than the first part. It lasts for four measures. There is a 4-measure introduction at the beginning of the tune that comes from the B section.

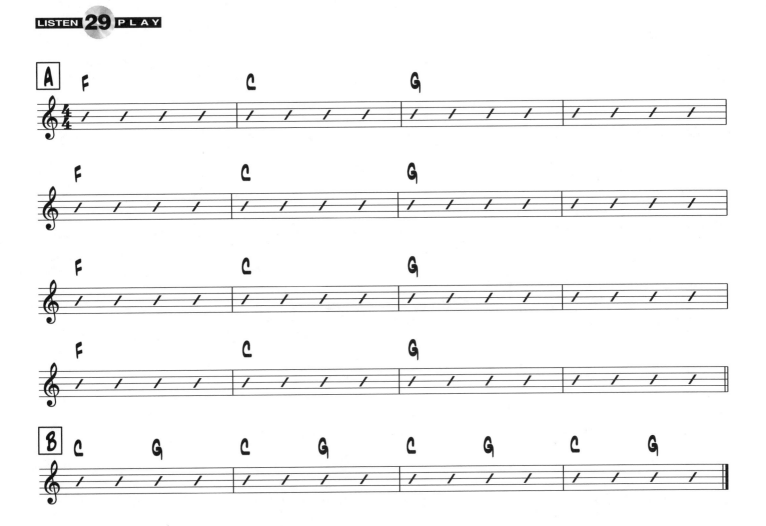

What is the arrangement on the recording? Figure it out by ear, and then check your answer against the summary at the end of this chapter.

IDEAS FOR IMPROVISING

Scale

The G major pentatonic scale will work well for the A section of this tune:

The G minor pentatonic scale will work well for the B section of this tune:

CALL AND RESPONSE

1. Echo each phrase, exactly as you hear it.
2. Improvise an answer to each phrase. Imitate the sound and rhythmic feel of the phrase you hear, and use the notes from the G pentatonic scales.

LISTEN **32** PLAY

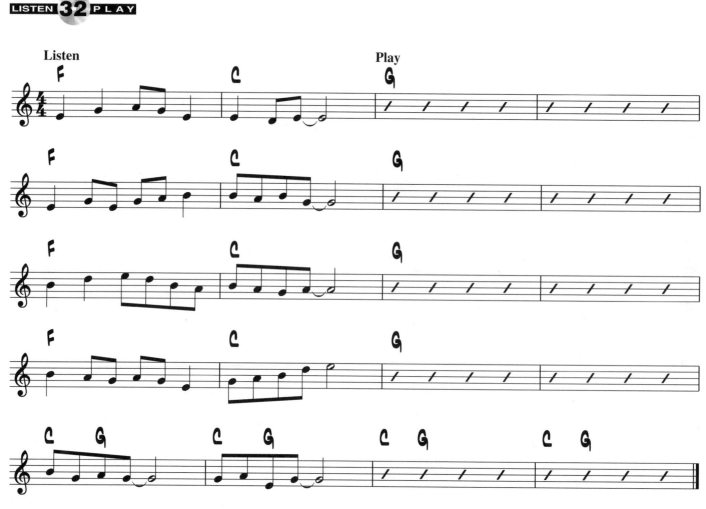

Listen   **Play**

Write out a few of your own ideas.

Create a one-chorus solo using any techniques you have learned. Memorize your solo and practice it along with the recording.

LESSON 24
READING

KEYBOARD PART

Play "Don't Look Down" along with the recording. Use the written keyboard part.

 First and second ending markings. The first time you play these measures, play the *first ending*—the measures under the number 1.

Then return to the begin-repeat sign (‖:). The second time, skip the first ending and play the *second ending*—the measures under the number 2. Then, continue through the rest of the form.

DON'T LOOK DOWN

By Matt Marvuglio

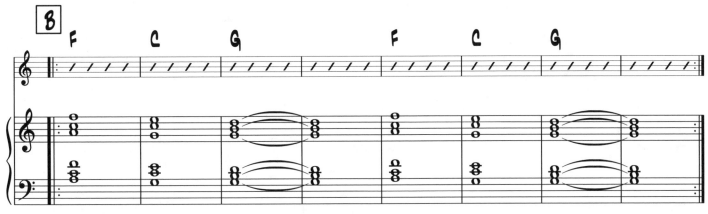

LEAD SHEET

This lead sheet shows the bass/guitar riff (see the ending), which you can double with low notes in your left hand.

PRACTICE TIP

When you play from a lead sheet, use it to help you keep your place. Even when you keep repeating the same comping patterns, follow along with the melody and chords as they are played by other instruments.

CHAPTER VI
DAILY PRACTICE ROUTINE

INVERSIONS

These are the inversions to the chords in "Don't Look Down." Practice them in all octaves.

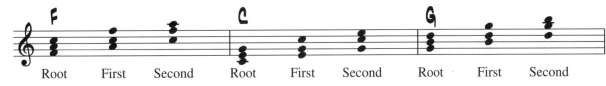

Practice this inversion exercise with the recording.

COMPING RHYTHMS

Practice comping to "Don't Look Down" using each of these rhythmic phrases. Create your own variations and practice along with the recording. Hook up with the groove.

LISTEN **34** PLAY

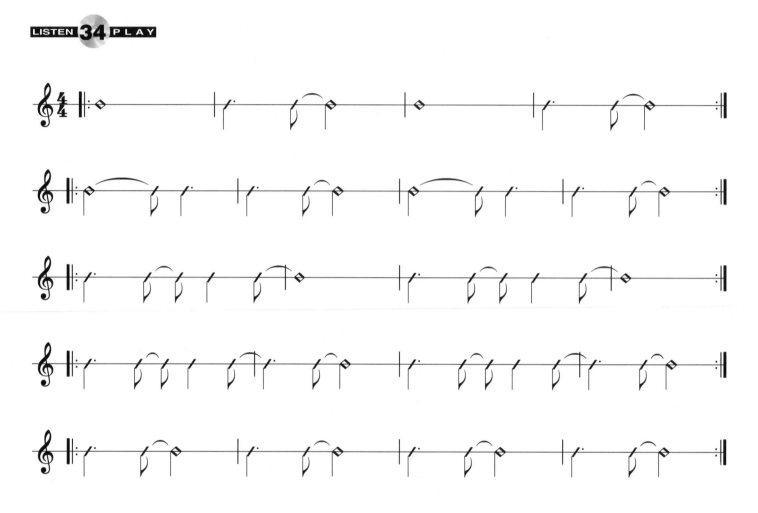

IMPROVISATION

Play a pad comping part in your left hand while you improvise with your right hand. Play several choruses, and try a variety of approaches. Use G major and minor pentatonic scales, the licks you studied in this chapter, and licks that you improvise while you are playing.

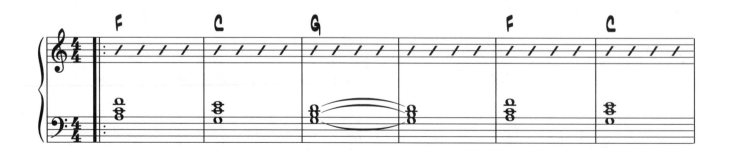

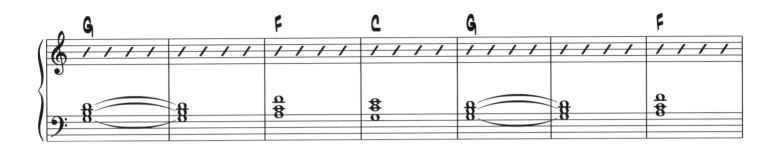

MEMORIZE

LISTEN **34** PLAY

Create your own comping part and improvised solo to "Don't Look Down." Practice it along with the recording, and memorize it.

Summary

Form
20-Bar AB form
(1 chorus = 20 bars)
A: 16 m.
B: 4 m.

Arrangement
Intro: 4 m.
1 Chorus Melody
1 Chorus Solo
1 Chorus Melody
End: 2 m.

Harmony

Scale

Play "Don't Look Down" with your own band!

"Take Your Time" is a *bossa nova* tune. Bossa nova began in Brazil, combining American jazz and an Afro-Brazilian form of dance music called *samba*. To hear more bossa nova, listen to Stan Getz, Antonio Carlos Jobim, Eliane Elias, Astrud Gilberto, Flora Purim, Dave Valentine, and Spyro Gyra.

LESSON 25
TECHNIQUE/THEORY

Listen to "Take Your Time" and then play along with the recording. Try to match the keyboard part. In this tune, you will play three comping patterns.

LISTEN **35** PLAY

First Comping Pattern

Second Comping Pattern

Third Comping Pattern

Play "Take Your Time" along with the recording, and try to match the keyboard part. Notice that all three phrases share the same rhythm.

CHORDS

The comping patterns in this tune each use a *passing chord*. This chord connects two inversions of the comping pattern's primary chord.

The first pattern is based on the **D–7** chord (the root D is played by the bass). The triads in the right hand use different inversions, which are indicated below the staff. The passing chord (circled) in this example is the II chord of D minor, **E–7**.

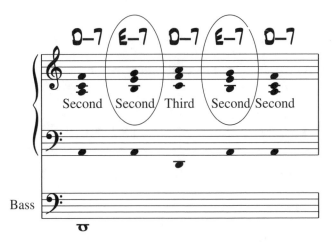

This is the same technique you saw in the blues chapters, when you used the IV chord. Passing chords help make comping patterns more melodic. Since they are generally not held for a very long time, they don't change the harmonic sound of the part.

Play the other two comping patterns of this tune and notice the use of passing chords.

LESSON 26
LEARNING THE GROOVE

HOOKING UP TO BOSSA NOVA

LISTEN **35** PLAY

Listen to "Take Your Time." This tune is a bossa nova, a style of music that originated in Brazil. Throughout the tune, a 2-bar rhythmic pattern repeats. This repeating pattern is an essential part of bossa nova. The drum plays it on a rim click.

Repeating rhythmic structures are at the heart of much African-based music, including Afro-Caribbean and most South and Latin American styles.

Find the pulse, and tap quarter notes with your left hand and eighth notes with your right hand. Remember that the eighth notes are played straight, not swing style.

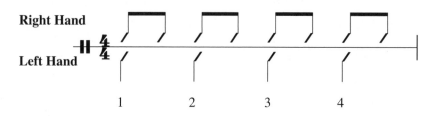

Next, accent the eighth notes as shown. This will be the essential part of your comping rhythm.

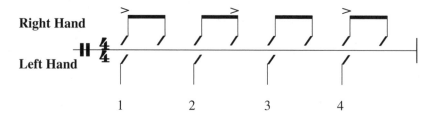

Now, tap only the accented notes and you have the rhythm!

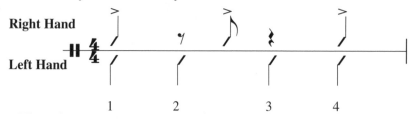

Finally, tap the entire comping rhythm.

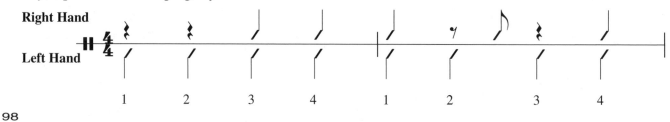

LESSON 27
IMPROVISATION

Listen to "Take Your Time" and try to figure out the form and arrangement by ear. Then continue with this chapter.

FORM AND ARRANGEMENT

This tune follows a 16-bar AB form. Each phrase of the melody lasts for eight measures.

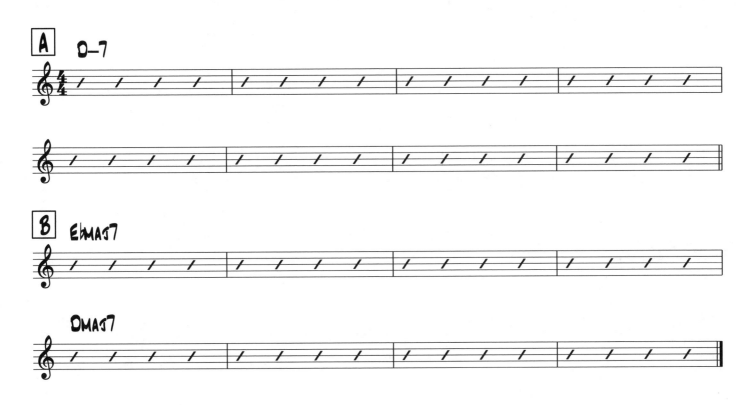

What is the arrangement on the recording? Figure it out by ear, and then check your answer against the summary at the end of this chapter.

IDEAS FOR IMPROVISING: SCALES

In this tune, try using two different scales when you improvise.

For the **D–7** and **E♭MAJ7** chords, use the D minor pentatonic scale:

For the last four measures, on the **DMAJ7** chord, use the D major pentatonic scale:

CALL AND RESPONSE

1. Echo each phrase, exactly as you hear it.
2. Improvise an answer to each phrase. Imitate the sound and rhythmic feel of the lick you hear, and use the notes from the D pentatonic scales.

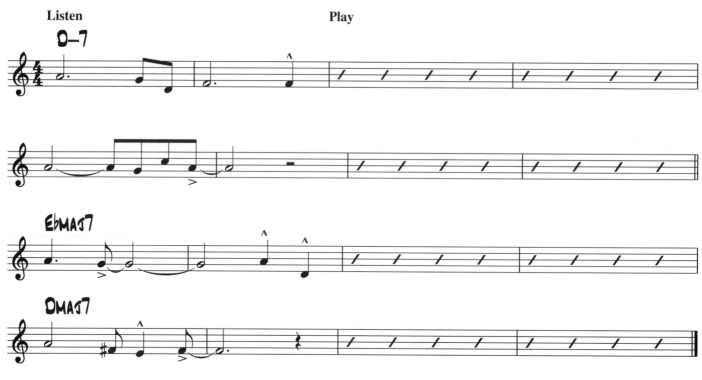

Listen   **Play**

Write out some of your own ideas. Use notes from the D pentatonic scales.

Create a one-chorus solo using any techniques you have learned. Memorize your solo and practice it along with the recording.

KEYBOARD PART

Play "Take Your Time" and use the written comping part.

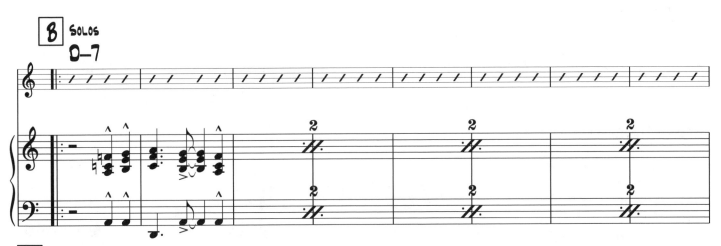

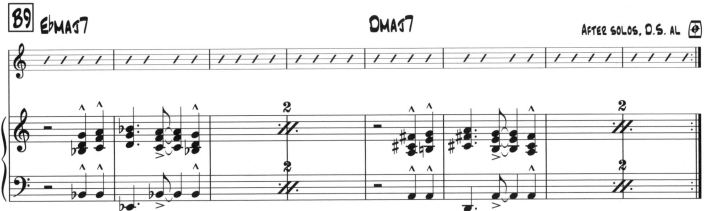

LEAD SHEET

Play "Take Your Time" and follow the lead sheet. Create your own comping part and practice it with the recording.

CHAPTER VII
DAILY PRACTICE ROUTINE

TECHNIQUE/THEORY

These are the inversions to the chords in "Take Your Time." Practice them in all octaves.

Practice this inversion exercise. As an added challenge, create your own left-hand accompaniment to the right-hand inversion exercise. Use your own rhythms for either part.

LISTEN **38** PLAY

Practice these comping variations, which begin on different inversions of the "Take Your Time" chords.

CHALLENGE

Create your own comping part using some of these inversions.

IMPROVISATION

There are many kinds of scales that you will eventually work into your improvising. These three scales are good resources for your improvisations. Throughout your career, you will learn many others and explore them in increasing depth.

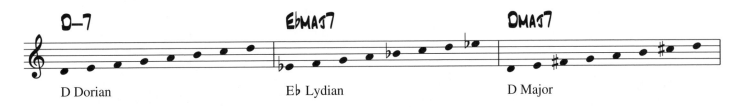

Play the root/seventh in your left hand while you play the scales with your right hand. Notice how different the scales sound, even though each begins on a "D." (When you are improvising, you can begin and end scales on any note.)

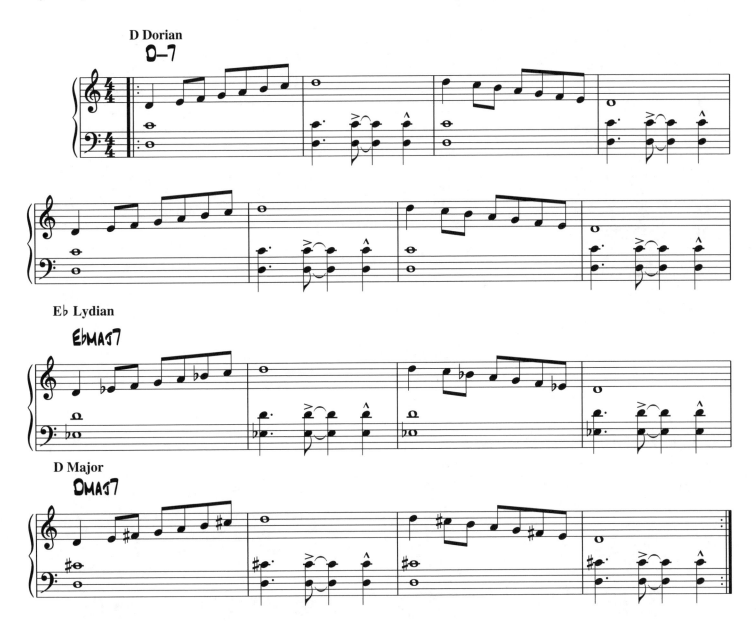

SCALE PRACTICE

You can use these three scales for improvisation ideas. Here is an example of a melody that uses the D Dorian scale.

Notice how different it looks and sounds when the notes are adjusted to fit the E♭MAJ7 chord, using E♭ Lydian:

And different still on DMAJ7, using D major:

Try writing your own melodic phrase and adjusting the notes as necessary to fit the other chords.

MEMORIZE

Create your own comping part and improvised solo to "Take Your Time." Practice it along with the recording, and memorize it.

SUMMARY

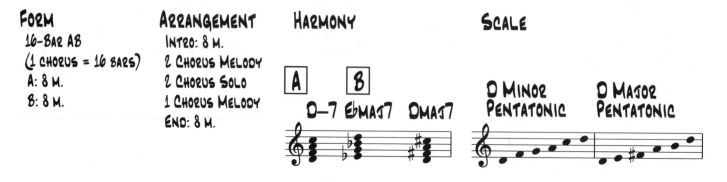

FORM	ARRANGEMENT	HARMONY	SCALE
16-BAR AB	INTRO: 8 M.		
(1 CHORUS = 16 BARS)	2 CHORUS MELODY		
A: 8 M.	2 CHORUS SOLO		
B: 8 M.	1 CHORUS MELODY		
	END: 8 M.		

PLAY "TAKE YOUR TIME" WITH YOUR OWN BAND!

"Stop It" is a blues/jazz tune in which *stop time* accents the melody, like a question and answer. Stop time is very common in blues, jazz, and other styles. To hear more stop time blues, listen to artists such as Miles Davis, John Coltrane, Jim Hall, Sarah Vaughn, Bill Evans, Ella Fitzgerald, Louis Armstrong, Abbie Lincoln, Dizzy Gillespie, and Charlie Parker.

CHAPTER VIII

LESSON 29
TECHNIQUE/THEORY

Listen to "Stop It" and then play along with the recording. Try to match the keyboard part. Notice that the comping rhythm changes during the solos. At the head, you will play three comping patterns. For the solo choruses, use the same chords, and follow your ear to match the new rhythm.

First Comping Pattern

Second Comping Pattern

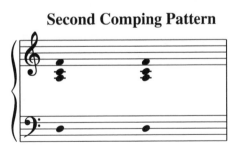

Third Comping Pattern

SHARP-NINTH CHORDS (♯9)

The chord in the third comping pattern has a different sound than any chord we have seen so far. It is a variation of an E7 chord that includes the sharp-ninth scale degree. Its chord symbol is **E7(♯9)**.

To understand how this chord works, start by playing an E7 chord.

Now, play the notes one by one, and add the ninth. Add each note slowly, holding the damper pedal down so that you can hear the notes ringing together. Listen for the added richness and color that the ninth adds to the chord sound.

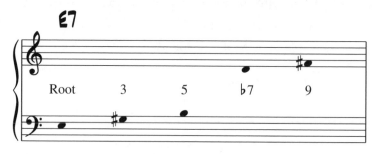

Since the chord symbol says (♯9), raise that ninth by half a step. The F-sharp becomes F-double-sharp, or G.

The voicing of this chord used on the recording of "Stop It" omits the fifth. This creates an open, dissonant sound, which is also very common in funk styles.

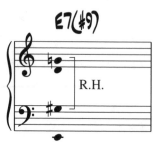

VOICING PRACTICE

Listen to the sound quality of **E7(♯9)**, compared to the other chords in "Stop It." Play the root with your left hand and all other notes with your right hand.

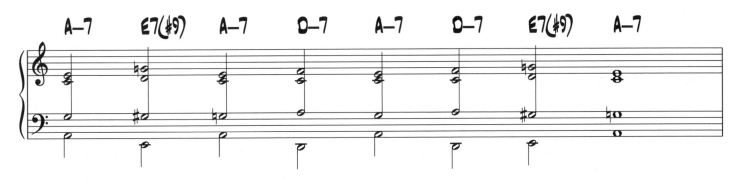

VOICE LEADING PRACTICE

Practice different voice leading for these chords, beginning on different inversions of **A–7**. When you play this tune with your own band, you will choose inversions and registers based on which other instruments are present, and what parts they are playing. Practicing a variety of options will help you become more versatile and creative.

> ### PRACTICE TIP
>
> When you are learning new chords and new tunes, practice them "out of time," moving from one chord to the next without playing rhythms. This is also a good way to experiment with different voicings and fingerings.

LESSON 30
LEARNING THE GROOVE

HOOKING UP TO STOP-TIME BLUES

LISTEN 39 PLAY

Listen to "Stop It." This jazz cymbal beat is at the heart of jazz rhythm. The "spang spang a-lang" cymbal beat is unique to jazz, and it has been its primary pattern since the 1940s. Its underlying pulse is the same as the shuffle. This pattern has accompanied Louis Armstrong, Count Basie, Miles Davis, John Coltrane, Duke Ellington, and thousands of other jazz artists.

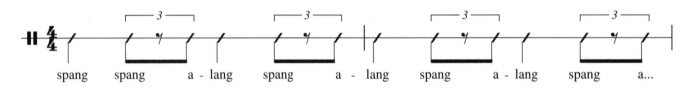

In stop time, the groove is punctuated by *stop-time kicks*. These are rhythmic figures, usually just one or two beats long, that punctuate the melody. That is why it is called "stop time"—the melody "stops" or rests. It is very important that you keep an accurate pulse through these areas where you do not play. Since the accented eighth note is an anticipated third beat, it makes sense to start counting on 4.

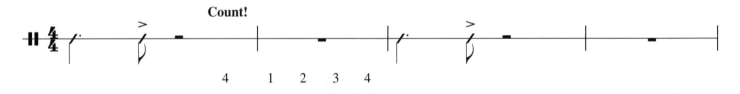

Let's look at the comping rhythm for the stop time melody chorus. Find the pulse and tap quarter notes with your left hand and swing eighth notes with your right hand.

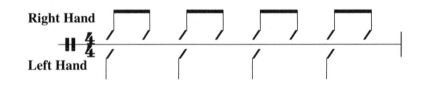

Next, accent the first and fourth eighth notes.

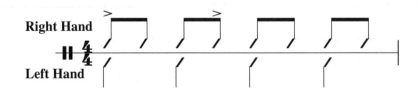

Then tap only the accented notes.

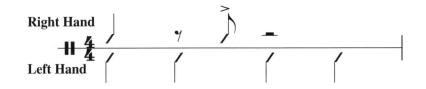

IMPROVISATION CHORUSES

During the solos, the rhythm section *plays time*. The drums play a steady beat and the bass walks. The comping patterns span two measures.

On this exercise, tap quarter notes with your left hand, and the top line with your right hand. Practice until you can "feel" where the comping rhythm's three attacks go.

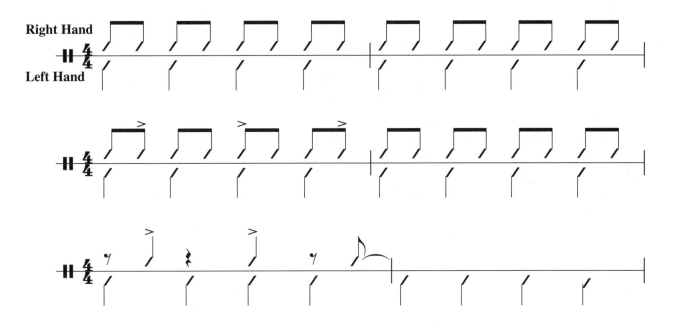

LESSON 31
IMPROVISATION

FORM AND ARRANGEMENT

Listen to "Stop It" and try to figure out the form and arrangement by ear. Check your answer against the summary at the end of this chapter.

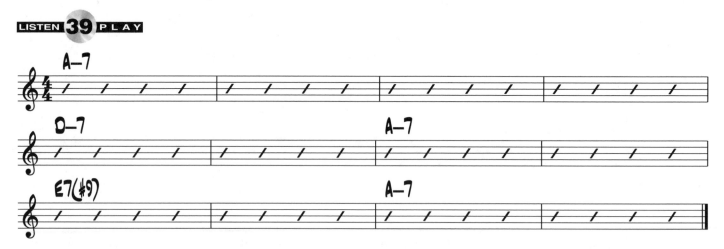

IDEAS FOR IMPROVISING

Use the A blues scale to improvise over this tune.

CALL AND RESPONSE

1. Echo each phrase, exactly as you hear it.
2. Improvise an answer to each phrase. Imitate the sound and rhythmic feel of the phrase you hear, and use the notes from the A blues scale.

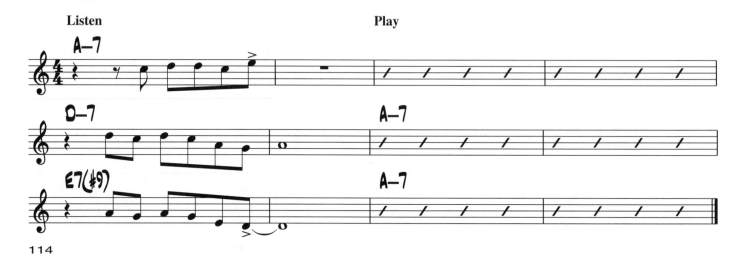

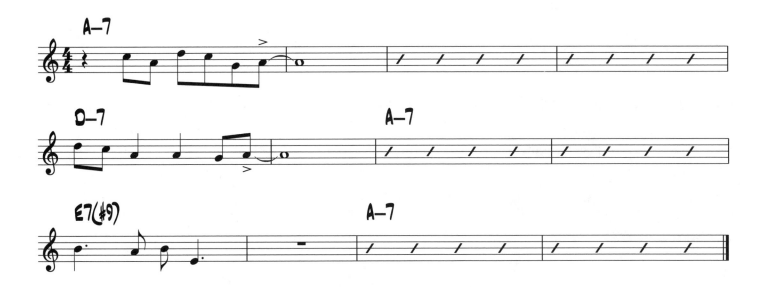

Write out a few of your own ideas. Use the A blues scale.

Create a one-chorus solo using any techniques you have learned. Memorize your solo and practice it along with the recording.

LESSON 32
READING

KEYBOARD PART

D.C. AL 🔶 From the beginning, and take the coda. Jump to the very first measure of the tune, and play from there. When you reach the first coda symbol, skip ahead to the next coda symbol (at the end). This is similar to the "**D.S. AL** 𝄋," but instead of going to a sign, go to the first measure of the tune.

Play "Stop It" along with the recording and read from the written keyboard part.

LISTEN **42** PLAY

STOP IT
KEYBOARD PART

BY MATT MARVUGLIO

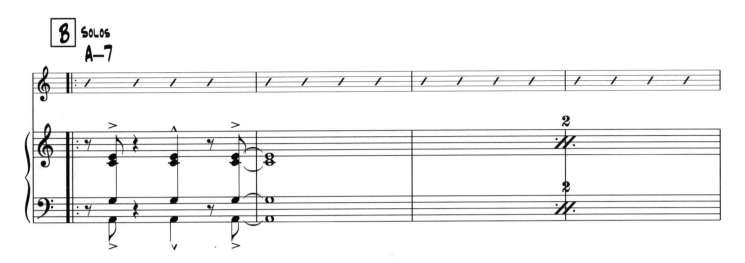

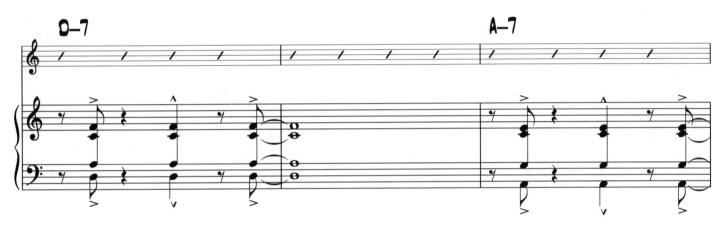

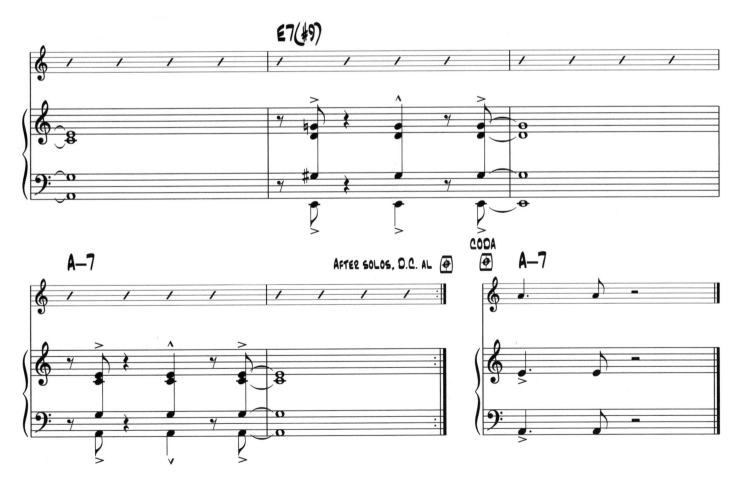

LEAD SHEET

Play "Stop It" from the lead sheet. Use your own comping part.

STOP IT

BY MATT MARVUGLIO

CHAPTER VIII
DAILY PRACTICE ROUTINE

TECHNIQUE/THEORY

Inversion Practice

Play this inversion exercise along with the recording.

LISTEN **42** PLAY

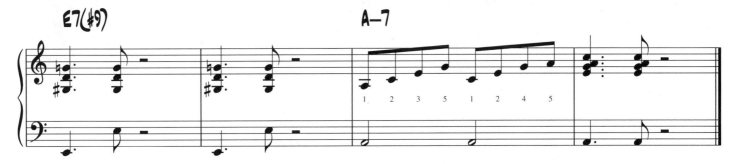

Pentatonic Practice 1

Even though pentatonic scales have five notes, they are often used in groups of four, as this grouping will fit better into $\frac{4}{4}$ time—groupings of fours, eights, etc.

Practice these 4-note groupings slowly until the shapes become comfortable. Notice that the suggested fingering treats each group as a separate phrase and makes no attempt to connect one group to another.

Pentatonic Practice 2

As these groups become more comfortable, try to increase the speed. When you are ready, play them as eighth notes with the recording. Also, try it with chords in your left hand.

Pentatonic Practice 3

Below is a 4-measure melody that uses only notes from the A minor pentatonic scale. If this phrase is stated three times, it will follow the blues form of twelve measures divided into three 4-measure phrases. Practicing this will help you develop a sense of the form and phrasing of the blues.

Create your own 4-measure phrase that repeats over the blues form. Use the A blues scale.

IMPROVISATION

Play comping chords in your left hand while you improvise with your right hand. Play several choruses, and try a variety of comping rhythms. In your right hand, use the blues scale, chord tones, licks from the melody, and any other techniques you have learned. Develop your solo, and then practice it along with the recording.

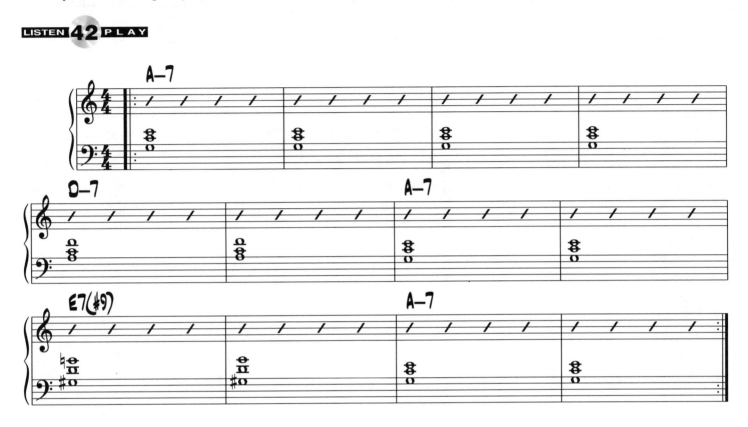

MEMORIZE

Create your own comping part and improvised solo to "Stop It." Practice it along with the recording, and memorize it.

SUMMARY

FORM	ARRANGEMENT	HARMONY	SCALE
12-BAR BLUES (1 CHORUS = 12 BARS)	2 CHORUS MELODY 4 CHORUS SOLO 2 CHORUS MELODY END: 1 M.	A-7 D- E7(#9)	A BLUES

PLAY "STOP IT" WITH YOUR OWN BAND!

FINAL REMARKS

Congratulations on completing the *Berklee Practice Method*. You now have a good idea of the role of the keyboardist in the band, and have command of the eight grooves and time feels of these tunes. The chords, voicings, and harmonic progressions that you have learned are important and useful parts of your musical vocabulary. In addition, you have tools and ideas for creating your own comping patterns and solos. This is a great start!

What to do next? Play along with your favorite recordings. Find records that you hear other musicians talking about. Learn these tunes, grooves, and comping patterns. There is a good reason that musicians talk about certain bands, albums, or keyboardists. Continue your theory, reading and technique work. Investigate chord scales and modes. Learn all your key signatures (major and minor), scales, and arpeggios.

Develop your concept of what it means to play keyboard. Realize how important you are as a keyboardist in a band. You have a big responsibility, taking care of both the groove and the harmony. It is a powerful position.

Play your keyboard every day, by yourself and with others, and get the sound in your body.

Keep the beat!

—Paul and Russ

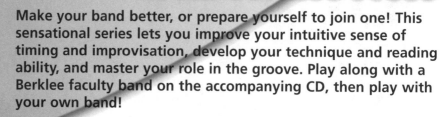

Berklee Press DVDs: Just Press PLAY

Record, Produce, Mix, Remix.
Repeat as necessary.

berklee press
AS SERIOUS ABOUT MUSIC AS YOU ARE

Recording and Producing in the Home Studio: A Complete Guide
By David Franz

Learn the basics of producing, setting up your studio, MIDI production techniques, editing tips, and how to mix and master.

ISBN: 0-87639-048-3
HL: 50448045

BOOK
$24.95

The Musician's Internet
By Peter Spellman

Learn to reach new audiences, expand your online presence, and attract thousands of new fans. A must for any self-managed musician.

ISBN: 0-634-03586-X
HL: 50449527

BOOK
$24.95

Producing Music with Digital Performer
By Ben Newhouse

Unlock all the power of Digital Performer to compose, record, and produce your music. Learn why DP is the tool of choice for so many music makers.

ISBN: 0-87639-056-4
HL: 50448050

BOOK/CD-ROM
$29.95

Mix Masters
Platinum Engineers Reveal Their Secrets for Success
By Maureen Droney

You'll find practical and informative behind-the-scenes, behind-the-glass insight into the art of mixing by the industry's most in-demand engineers across all genres—pop, rock, country, classical, and film.

ISBN: 0-87639-019-X
HL: 50448023

BOOK
$24.95

Producing in the Home Studio with Pro Tools: Second Edition
By David Franz

This comprehensive home-studio guide will show you how to create the highest-quality recordings by teaching you fundamental production skills and engineering techniques.

The new second edition has been updated for Pro Tools 6. It also covers all the new Digidesign home studio hardware, including Digi 002, Mbox, and Digi 001—and shows you how to use it effectively. CD-ROM includes Pro Tools session templates and MP3s.

ISBN: 0-87639-008-4
HL: 50449526

BOOK/CD-ROM
$34.95

The Complete Guide to Remixing
By Erik Hawkins

A comprehensive handbook of the history, technology, craft, and art of remixing. Learn cutting-edge tips on using today's hottest software, including Pro Tools, Sonar, and Reason.

ISBN: 0-87639-044-0
HL: 50448030

BOOK/CD
$29.95

Arranging in the Digital World
By Corey Allen

Great for beginners! Create truly inspired digital arrangements using today's electronic and digital instruments. Teaches basic sequencing and production concepts, with step-by-step directions for building MIDI arrangements in any style.

ISBN: 0-634-00634-7
HL: 50449415

BOOK/ MIDI DISK
$19.95

Finale®: An Easy Guide to Music Notation
By Thomas E. Rudolph and Vincent A. Leonard, Jr.

The indispensable resource for learning to use this most powerful music notation software program. Master all of Finale's capabilities with step-by-step instructions. Compatible for both Macintosh and Windows computer platforms.

ISBN: 0-634-01666-0
HL: 50449501

BOOK/CD-ROM
$59.95

Recording in the Digital World
By Thomas E. Rudolph and Vincent A. Leonard, Jr.

Build the perfect digital studio, no matter what your budget. Includes advice and recommendations on studio equipment, software, and the latest technologies, plus practical tips for creating, editing, and mastering a digital recording.

ISBN: 0-634-01324-6
HL: 50449472

BOOK
$29.95

Remix
Berklee In the Pocket series
By Erik Hawkins

A handy, practical guide to recent advances in personal computer technology and music software programs that allow practically any song, regardless of its original tempo, to be remixed.

ISBN: 0-87639-058-0
HL: 50448054

BOOK
$9.95

berklee press

Berklee Press books and DVDs are available wherever music books are sold.
Go to www.berkleepress.com or call 866-BERKLEE (237-5533) for a complete catalog of Berklee Press products.

DISTRIBUTED BY

HAL•LEONARD®